BIG
QUESTIONS

STEVE LEGG

First published in Great Britain 1999 by
Breakout Publishing

British Library Cataloguing in Publication Data
A record for this book is available from the British Library

ISBN 1-901796-12-4

Designed and typeset by
Christian Publicity Organisation, Worthing.

Printed and bound in Great Britain by
Cox & Wyman Ltd, Reading, Berks.

Breakout Publishing is a division of
The Breakout Trust
PO Box 3070, Littlehampton
West Sussex BN17 5AW
publishing@breakout.org.uk

In loving memory of
Allan Botting

Allan was a wonderful friend, a great
encourager and supporter of mine.
He enjoyed reading my books
(what impeccable taste he had!),
though never had a chance to see this one
in print, as he unexpectedly went home to
be with Jesus on the
15th July 1999.

Someone once said that heaven is
a place prepared for those who are
prepared for it. I know Allan was
prepared. Are you?

Contents

About the Author

Steve Legg is an evangelist, escapologist, author and Director of The Breakout Trust, a UK-based charity committed to communicating the relevance of the Christian faith. This is done through a variety of ways including magic and escapology. Dangerous and daring escapes suspended from cranes or manacled between high-powered jeeps going in opposite directions have brought massive attention to Steve's abilities to draw and entertain large crowds across the world.

As well as entertaining, though, Steve often uses his skills to communicate a powerful message of freedom through Christianity. Steve talks and demonstrates his talents in schools, colleges, universities, pubs, night clubs and out onto the streets, from Portland Prison to Canterbury Cathedral—in fact wherever people are.

As a Guinness World Record holder, Steve travels the length and breadth of the country, as well as working in various countries across the world. He has been privileged to work with a whole list of household names including Jonathan Ross, Gloria

Hunniford, Fern Britton, Paul Ross, Helen Shapiro, Gloria Gaynor, Boyzone, Roger Whittaker, Zoe Ball, Keith Chegwin, Phillipa Forrester, top Radio 1 D.J. Mark Radcliffe and the boy 'Lard,' Don Maclean, Lorraine Chase and Brit-Pop Band, Republica, to name just a few!

He has appeared on national television on numerous occasions, and his impressive list of TV credits include 'How 2,' 'The Big Breakfast,' and 'The Disney Club' right through to 'Songs of Praise'. In 1995, Steve was part of the 'Cannon and Ball Gospel Show' that toured the UK. This major tour covered a staggering 48 dates across the nation, making it one of the biggest Gospel tours ever produced. The show was also the subject for a BBC special documentary, and became the number one best-selling video of its kind.

On top of all this, Steve is also an accomplished presenter, broadcaster and writer. He has written a number of small booklets for CPO, the Christian literature charity based in Worthing. His first paperback, 'Making Friends—Evangelism the Easy Way' was written for Christians equipping them to share their faith more effectively. Then 'Man, Myth or Maybe More?' was released in March 1999, which examined the life of Jesus, from his birth in a smelly shed, through a life full of incredible occurrences, to his death at the hands of his fellow countrymen and onto the greatest comeback of all time.

He is married to Jemma, and has three small children, Jay, Amber and Emmie, and they are all part of Arun Community Church in Littlehampton, West Sussex. Steve is also a member of the Rustington Sports and Social Club, Equity, London's prestigious Magic Circle and a very proud member of The Curry Club.

Acknowledge-ments

This book would never have happened without the help of so many friends. I'm going to have a go at naming them all, but if I forget anyone, then please forgive me!

To Paul and Jane Archer, Tim and Anita Ball, Allan and Meem Bernau, Steve and Lyn Burnhope, Mary Botting, Heidi Campion, Paul and Margaret Crocombe, Ian and Janet Duncan, Andy and Annette Economides, Steve and Luz Gale, Pete and Jane Harris, Nathan Lock, Betty Longman, Jonathan and Liz McClelland, Will and Clare Palmer, David and Meg Pritchard, Neil and Clare Sharples, Paul Sinclair and the Church on the High Road, Steve and Cilla Sparks, Jeff and Audrey Travis, and Roger Gooderidge. I couldn't be doing what I'm doing without your regular support. Thanks a million.

Also to those who helped make the book happen: Syd Little, Chris Gidney, Sally Goring from Christians in Entertainment (you're really appreciated Sally), Alan Mullery, Dave Bemment, John Forrest and Gerald Williams. Thank you so much for your help and contributions.

Finally to Bob Bond for his excellent illustrations (yet again), and indeed all the gang at CPO in Worthing, you beauties!! Andy Webb (Ace Journalist) thanks for proof-reading the book—if you spot any mistakes blame him, not me!! Finally, to Alan and Nicole Snuggs and Roy and Pat Jones who have lent me useful reference books when I've stayed in their homes, thanks to you too. The cheques are in the post!

Foreword

We're certainly surrounded by questions, and as the popular song says, 'There are more questions than answers.' I've certainly found this to be true in my life, but I've also found the answers to some of my questions, particularly when thinking about faith.

I've had a life in showbusiness full of glamour, but I've also known private pain and personal crisis. It was during some of these difficulties that my search for spiritual answers intensified, and I discovered that there really was a God who cared for me as an individual. He not only heard my prayers, but answered them too!

Of course I still enjoy being part of a famous comedy duo. 'Little and Large' has played a big role in my life for the past thirty years. However, I also put aside some time these days to chat and sing in pubs, clubs and churches about my revitalised Christian faith. These evenings are great fun, are filled with laughter and tears and give me a chance to personally explain how important my faith in God has become.

Remembering how someone once said that God made each of us like a jigsaw with a God-shaped piece missing, reminds me of the spiritual search that so many are fervently involved in. Somehow we feel that part of us is not completed, yet a deep question awaits an answer. Many in my business try to fill the missing piece with 'sex, drugs and rock 'n' roll', but I've found that it is only God who can successfully fill the gap and provide real answers.

I know that if we had all the answers, we would be God ourselves, but I am satisfied that he has provided us with enough evidence to point us in the right direction. I pray that as you read Steve Legg's book you will be excited to find some answers too.

Introduction

After Shakespeare, Samuel Johnson is possibly the best known figure and the most frequently quoted in the whole range of English literature. He was a poet, critic, essayist and lexicographer, so I guess he knew a thing or two! It was Samuel Johnson who said: "curiosity is one of the permanent and certain characteristics of a vigorous intellect." So, you must be pretty bright to have started reading the book in the first place!

'Big Questions' surprisingly enough is all about questions, and trying to answer them. Life just seems to be full of questions. Let's look at just some of the great mysteries of our time, right here and now...

Why are shoes in a sale never available in your size?

If Barbara Cartland is the world's best-selling author, why can't you name one of her books?

If all the world is a stage where does the audience sit?

Why is it that when your train is late, the bus you have to catch from the station will be on time?

Why is it that when you're poor enough to need a bank loan, you're too bad a risk to get one?

Why do floorboards only creak at night?

How do you throw away a dustbin?

Why is it, that whichever queue you join, the other one will move faster?

Why do butterflies only live a short time when eating cabbage is meant to be so healthy?

Why do you never have the correct change for vending machines?

Why do cream crackers always break into three when you bite them?

Why does coffee always smell better than it tastes?

Why is it considered necessary to nail down the lid of a coffin?

Why did Shakespeare use so many famous quotations?

Questions, questions, questions! In writing this book, I can associate with the American movie star, Douglas Fairbanks, Jr., who started an important lecture by saying: "I feel like a mosquito in a nudist colony. I look around and I know it's wonderful to be here, but I don't know where to begin."

I know what's he trying to say! I almost didn't know where to start, though I obviously had to start somewhere. So, in this book we'll bypass some of the daft ones listed above, and instead take a look at some of the important questions in life. Real tough ones like; where do you fit in, the universe and everything, and do you matter?

They really are big questions. They deserve big answers—in fact so big that God and Jesus come into them, and that's what this book is about. In a very simple way I'm going to try to address and attempt to answer the questions that really matter. Not with religious, out-of-date mumbo jumbo but with down-to-earth common sense, and some extra special good news thrown in for good measure!

ONE

Who made God?

WHEN I WAS AT SCHOOL I always used to have an image of God, as an old Father Christmas lookalike, with a bushy white beard, going thin on top and wearing a Marks and Spencer nightshirt. I don't know what images are conjured up in your mind? Maybe they're similar, maybe not. But if there is a God in heaven somewhere, how on earth did he get there? And for that matter, who made him?

The answer's short and sweet. No-one! I believe God's always been there and always will be there. In the eighteenth century the philosopher Jean Jacques Rousseau attempted to describe it like this: "I know nothing of his having created matter, bodies, spirits or the world. The idea of creation confounds me and surpasses my conception, though I believe as much of it as I am able to conceive. But I know that God has formed

the universe and all that exists, in the most consummate order. He is doubtless eternal, but I am incapacitated to conceive an idea of eternity. All that I can conceive is, that he existed before all things, that he exists with them and will exist after them, if they should ever have an end."

Now the statement that God has always been there and will always be there, might be a bit of a strange concept to get our tiny minds around. After all, everything needs to be created. Well yes, that's certainly true for physical things; like the chair I'm sitting on at this very minute, or the keyboard that I'm thumping away at to write this book. But the Bible says God is spiritual not physical. 'He was there before anything was made, and all things continue because of him.' (Colossians 1:17)

So, it's not outside the realms of possibility to suggest that spiritual beings don't have to obey physical laws, and in fact exist totally outside of these laws. Professor Sir Ghillean Prance, the Director of the Royal Botanical Gardens at Kew in London said: "Physical laws came into being because there is a Creator who made them."

I've got to admit that this all seems a bit peculiar. Indeed the whole concept of things existing outside of time and space was virtually dismissed until Albert Einstein came along with his theory of relativity. That theory might make it a little easier to understand the Bible's teaching about God existing outside of time and space as we know it.

I hope that this has given part of an answer to this tricky question. Let me leave the last word to Andre Gide, the French Nobel Prize winning author who said this: "I cannot tell where God begins, still less where he ends. But my belief is better expressed if I say that there is no end to God's beginning."

What is God like?

I WAS WATCHING MY SON, Jay, aged six, engrossed in drawing a picture. I asked him what he was drawing. "It's a picture of God", he said. "Mm, that's interesting son," I replied. "No-one really knows what God looks like." Jay looked up at me, then carried on with his masterpiece and said very matter-of-factly: "They will do in a few minutes."

None of us knows what God is like. I mentioned before my particular image of God, where he looks like Father Christmas with a long beard, receding hair, red rosy cheeks, floating on a white fluffy cloud, wearing long flowing robes whilst strumming away on a little gold harp. Others view him as a mysterious, impersonal cosmic 'force,' or maybe as a bitter and severe authoritarian Sergeant-Major type who wants to stop us having fun.

Are any of these views accurate, I wonder? The Bible doesn't have any pictures or photographs of God, but it does say that people were made in the 'image and likeness of God.' (Genesis 1:26). This kind of description is given the technical name of 'anthropomorphism,' which is taken from anthropos, 'man' and morphe, which means 'shape.' That all sounds a bit technical, so lets take a look beyond what we feel God physically looks like, to what he is like, and some of his characteristics.

Around 3000 years ago, David, who was a King

himself, described God like this: "Lord you are great and powerful. You have glory, victory and honour. Everything in heaven belongs to you. The kingdom belongs to you, Lord; You are the ruler over everything." (1 Chronicles 29:11) Now that's pretty powerful! Elsewhere, the Old Testament uses vivid language to describe him. We're told God is: love, light, eternal, perfect, wise, the high and lofty one, the holy one of Israel. He's also described as the rock, a fortress, a shepherd, a bridegroom and the list goes on and on.

The emphasis changes slightly in the New Testament where God is described as 'Father.' In Biblical days a Jewish father ruled, provided and cared for his family. Paul, an important New Testament church leader described Christians as 'adopted' children of God, that God had bought, 'so we could become his children.' (Galatians 4:5). Paul went on to encourage us to call God 'Abba' (and I'm not talking about the seventies Swedish Supergroup!), the most intimate Jewish family word, literally Daddy. That's a great picture of God, a heavenly Dad who loves and cares, and wants the best for us.

The American author, Philip Yancey, described it like this: "People grow up with all sorts of notions of what God is like. They see God as an Enemy, or a Policeman, or even an Abusive Parent. Or perhaps they do not see God at all and only hear his silence. Because of Jesus, however, we no longer have to wonder how God feels or what he is like. When in doubt, we can look at Jesus to correct our blurry vision."

How can you believe in something you can't see?

EUGENE CERNAN, one of the American astronauts who enjoyed the exciting experience of walking on the moon, said with wonder as he looked at our planet from space: "Our world appears big and beautiful, all blue and white! You can see from the Antarctic to the North Pole. The earth looks so perfect. There are no strings to hold it up; there is no fulcrum upon which it rests." Contemplating the infinity of time and space, he said he felt as if he were seeing the earth from God's perspective. Christians believe, God is very real and wants to make a difference in your life.

As we've already said, you can't see God. Or, for that matter, taste, touch or smell him. But so what? Sometimes you just have to believe in things that you can't see. There's electricity, for example. You can't see it, though you can see the effect of it, when you turn on a light switch. Then there's radio waves—you just know when you turn on your radio that sound is going to come out. What about microwaves? You can't see those either, but I know full well that when I put my half-eaten, cold chicken vindaloo from the night before, into the microwave to heat up, five minutes later it's piping hot and goes down a treat!

In the same way, although we can't physically see God, we can see the effects of God all around us in the wonders of creation. For example, Jim Bishop's article, which follows here, says it much better than I could:

"There is no God. All of the wonders round us are accidental. No almighty hand made a thousand stars. They made themselves. No power keeps them on their steady course. The earth spins itself to keep the oceans from falling off towards the sun. Infants teach themselves to cry when they are hungry or hurt. A small flower invented itself so that we could extract digitalis for sick hearts.

The earth gave itself day and night, and tilted itself so that we get seasons. Without the magnetic poles man would be unable to navigate the trackless oceans of water and air, but they grew there. How about the sugar thermostat in the pancreas? It maintains a level of sugar in the blood sufficient for energy. Without it, all of us would fall into a coma and die.

Why does snow sit on mountain-tops waiting for the warm spring sun to melt it at just the right time for the young crops in farms below to drink? A very lovely accident.

The human heart will beat for seventy to eighty years or more without faltering. How does it get sufficient rest between beats? A kidney will filter poison from the blood, and leave good things alone. How does it know one from the other?

Who gave the human tongue flexibility to form words, and a brain to understand them, but denied it to animals? Who showed a womb how to take the love of two people and keep splitting a tiny ovum until, in time, a baby would have the proper number of fingers, eyes, ears and hair in the right places. Then come into the world when it is strong enough to sustain life?

There is no God?"

Enough said. I hope I've made my point.

FOUR

Did Jesus really exist?

BARRY NORMAN, the British film critic, made quite a profound statement when he was reviewing a movie about the life of Jesus. "Very few people could have as magnetic a personality as Christ, and no actor has that. You will always know you are looking at an actor pretending to be someone infinitely greater than he is....The whole point about Christ, if you believe in Christ, is that Christ is divine, not that he was a jolly good chap."

We know that Jesus lived. He was a man in history, as well as a man for today. Tacitus, perhaps the greatest Roman historian, born in the first century, speaks of Jesus. Josephus, a Jewish historian tells of the crucifixion of Jesus. A contemporary Bible scholar said that "the latest edition of the Encyclopaedia Britannica uses 20,000 words in describing this person, Jesus. His description took more space than was given to Aristotle, Cicero, Alexander, Julius Caesar, Buddha, Confucius, Mohammed or Napoleon Bonaparte."

Jesus was certainly something special. Let's look at just some of the evidence for his existence from three very different sources.

Jewish Historians

The most famous of these is Josephus who was born around AD 37 in Jerusalem. He devoted a large part of his life to writing numerous books on the history of the Jews. One of these, The Antiquities of The Jews said this:

"Now there was about this time Jesus a wise man, if it be lawful to call him a man; for he was a doer of wonderful works, a teacher of such men as received the truth with pleasure. He drew over to him many Jews, and also many of the Gentiles. This man was the Christ. And when Pilate had condemned him to the cross, those who had loved him from the first did not forsake him for he appeared to them alive on the third day, the divine prophets having spoken these and thousands of other wonderful things about him. And even now, the race of Christians, so named from him, has not died out." (Antiquities of The Jews, XVIII,III).

Pagan Writers

Would you believe it, they write about Jesus too. For example, Tacitus, a Roman historian in AD 112 writes about the reign of the Emperor Nero and refers to Jesus and the Christians in Rome. (Annals XV,44). Soon after this Pliny the Younger, once described as one of the world's great letter writers, writes an interesting letter about Christianity to the Emperor Trajan. In it he mentions the early Christians singing hymns, worshipping Jesus as God, pledging themselves not to do wicked things, but instead to live moral lives. This is what he said:

"They were in the habit of meeting on a certain fixed day before it was light, when they sang in alternate verses a hymn to Christ, as to a god, and bound themselves by a solemn oath, not to do any wicked deeds, never to commit any fraud, theft or adultery, never to falsify their word, nor deny a trust when they should be called upon to deliver it up."

The Bible

Many would automatically discount the Bible as a form of reliable evidence because of its bias towards the Christian faith, or because it maybe has been added to, or exaggerated over the years—almost like a version of 'Chinese Whispers'. But that's not so. Researchers in Israel, after subjecting the first five books of the Bible to exhaustive computer analysis, came to a different conclusion than even they had initially expected. Sceptics had long assumed the Torah (the first five books of the Bible) to have been the work of multiple authors and not, as Christians had always believed, the work of one man, Moses.

But Scripture scholar Moshe Katz and computer expert

Menachem Wiener of the Israel Institute of Technology discovered an intricate pattern of significant words in the books, spelled by letters separated at fixed intervals. The statistical possibilities of such patterns happening by chance would be one in three million. The material suggests a single, inspired author—in fact it could not have been put together by human capabilities at all. Mr. Wiener adds, "So we need a non-rational explanation, and ours is that the Torah was written by God through the hand of Moses."

The following anonymous piece seems to sum up how special and unique Jesus was:

"He was born in an obscure village, the child of a peasant woman. He grew up in yet another village, where he worked in a carpenter's shop until he was thirty. Then for three years he was an itinerant preacher.

He never wrote a book. He never held an office. He never had a family or owned a big house. He didn't go to college. He never travelled more than 200 miles from the place where he was born. He did none of the things one usually associates with greatness. He had no credentials but himself.

He was only thirty-three when the tide of public opinion turned against him. His friends ran away. He was nailed to a cross between two thieves. While he was dying, his executioners gambled for his clothing, the only property he had on earth.

Nineteen centuries have come and gone and today he is the central figure of the human race. All the armies that ever marched, all the navies that ever sailed, all the parliaments that have ever sat, all the kings that ever reigned, put together, have not affected the life of man on this earth as that one solitary life."

FIVE

Was Jesus actually born on December 25?

MANY YEARS AGO the land of Persia was ruled by a wise and beloved Shah who cared greatly for his people and desired only what was best for them. One day he disguised himself as a poor man and went to visit the public baths. The water for the baths was heated by a furnace in the cellar, so the Shah made his way to the dark place to sit with the man who was in charge of the fire. The two men shared a meagre meal, and the Shah befriended him in his loneliness, and day after day the ruler came to visit the man.

Eventually the Shah revealed his true identity, and he expected the man to ask him for money or a gift. Instead he looked long into his leader's face and, with love and wonder in his voice, said: "You left your palace and your glory to sit with me in this dark place, to eat my coarse food, and to care about what happens to me. On others you bestow riches and gifts, but to me you have given yourself."

Apparently that's a true story, and it wonderfully illustrates what happened that first Christmas, when God left heaven and came to earth as a man in the form of Jesus.

You might have expected the Son of Almighty God to have been born in a palace or a huge mansion, but he ended up coming into the world in a smelly little stable in a tiny town stuck in the middle of nowhere. The crowds in Bethlehem at that time didn't have an inkling that the Son of God was asleep in their little town. Indeed, at his actual birth, only a few simple shepherds came to see him. Yet they left different people, glorifying God, because the Saviour had been born. A statement

was being made here—Jesus had come for ordinary people, like you and me.

His birth occurred, of course, on 25 December AD1 ... or did it? Well, it might seem a bit daft, considering this was one of the most awesome moments in the whole history of the world, but we don't really know exactly when he was born. In fact, even the precise year is uncertain. It certainly wasn't in the year AD 1 as the calendar's Anno Domini (Year of the Lord) suggests.

The thing is, our dating system derived from an error about the year of Jesus' birth, made by a sixth-century monk in Rome, Dionysius Exigus, in working out the starting point of the Christian era. Scholars since have calculated that Jesus' birth happened about 5 or 7 BC (which of course means 'Before Christ'). The revised time was determined partly by the fact that Herod the Great ruled Judea when Jesus was born and the history books record that Herod died in March 4 BC.

As to what month the birth occurred, or on what day,

has been a matter of great speculation for many centuries. Possible dates include: 6 January, 2 February, 25 March, 19 April, 20 May, 4 October and 17 November. We do know for sure it certainly wasn't the 25 December.

A British physicist and astronomer, David Hughes, calculated that the date was 17 September, 7 BC, based on various scientific evidence, including that of a conjunction of two planets, Jupiter and Saturn, in the constellation of Pisces on that date. He concludes in a book that this extraordinary celestial display was the 'star' seen by the distant wise men. The 17th century German astronomer, Johannes Kepler, similarly had calculated a three-planet conjunction, including Venus as well as Jupiter and Saturn, in the same constellation in 7 BC.

Most scholars would now accept that Jesus was probably born around the middle of September in 5 BC, and the reason for our celebrations being based around the 25 December? Well, until the fourth century the 25 December was a pagan feast day to celebrate the power of the 'sun.' Then Constantine, the Roman Emperor at the time became a Christian and decided to turn that day into a feast day to celebrate the birth of the 'son' of God.

But for all the clouded chronology and background of that first Christmas, one fact is clear—that God entered the world as part of it and in love with it. You see Jesus is for life, not just for Christmas. American Rock singer Joan Osborne's song 'One of Us' was in the charts in 1996 for weeks, with some interesting lyrics. "What if God was one of us. Just a slob like one of us." I'm sure some religious people were offended by the insinuation that God was a slob. But I like the song and its sentiments. For God chose to come to earth as a human being, indeed a tiny baby who was born in a stinking stable.

That's what the first Christmas was all about. It wasn't about turkey, tinsel and toffees! No, it was that God left the splendour of heaven and came in flesh and blood to live with us for a while to make a difference.

SIX

Why was Jesus so special?

THE AMERICAN ASTRONAUT, James Irwin, was one of the few men to have experienced the sensation of walking on the moon. He said, "Jesus walking on the earth is far more important than man walking on the moon." Let's take a brief look at Jesus' time on earth and examine just a few of things that he said and did that made him so special:

He said we are all important

He once told a story about a farmer with 100 sheep who lost one of them. He left the 99 to look for the lost sheep. He was happier about finding that one sheep than the 99 that were never lost. In the same way God doesn't want any of us to be lost; he wants to find us and for us to find him, whoever and wherever we are.

Someone once said that if God had a wallet he would have your photo in it. He'd wander around heaven, proudly showing your picture to everyone he could find. It's a wonderful illustration (that I wish I'd thought of) that helps us realise God's love for each individual.

He said he was the only way to God

Jesus said, "I am the way, the truth and life. The only way to the Father is through me." (John 14:6) It could sound like an incredibly arrogant statement unless it really is true. The truth can sound a bit arrogant though; 5 + 5 =10, not 11, 9 or $10^1/2$. They're all close to the true answer, but they're not right. Do you see what I mean? Jesus' statement kind of dismisses the old statement that 'all roads somehow lead to God'.

Now certainly other religions have elements of truth and some great moral teaching, but look at those words of Jesus again, "...the way, the truth and the life...". Christianity is about people knowing God in a personal way through Jesus.

He healed people

Jesus' work began with teaching and healing. He didn't just talk about the power of God, he actually demonstrated it as well, and crowds from all over Palestine, not surprisingly, flocked to see him. One day in Capernaum, his disciple Peter told him about his mother-in-law who was suffering from a fever.Jesus touched her and the fever left immediately (Matthew 8:14-16).

Another day, as Jesus was healing people in a house, some men tried to bring in their paralysed friend to him. They couldn't get in because of the vast crowds so they went onto the roof and started to dig through the layers upon layers of clay, grass and branches to make a hole through which they could lower the man through the ceiling! Now that's what I call a pretty impressive entrance. Jesus saw them, and seeing their faith, healed him. (Luke 5: 17-26).

He also healed lepers, a deformed and withered hand, deafness and dumbness, blindness, a severed ear, bleeding and a disease called dropsy that caused the body to swell. The thing is, though, most of Jesus' miracles weren't even recorded, and the ones we know about are just some of the incredible things he did, to show God's wonderful compassion and love for people.

He turned water into wine

Being an interesting sort of person, Jesus got invited to a wedding and the party afterwards. He was there with his family and friends and then the organisers ran out of wine, a major problem! Unlike our short weddings today with the service over in an hour, and then a two hour reception, in Jesus' day it was quite a bit more than mushroom vol-au-vents, sausage rolls and a slice of cake! Weddings then usually took about a week. On the first day, the couple exchanged vows under a canopy, then for the next six days or more, the happy couple and all the guests celebrated with dancing, games, music, food and wine. It sounds quite a party doesn't it, and it was, until they ran out of wine! The Bible tells us Jesus went and found six jars of water, each holding around 100 litres and he miraculously turned the contents into the very best wine—I reckon it was over 900 bottles worth!

He fed thousands

There's a BBC Television cookery show I like very much, called, 'Ready, Steady, Cook', where contestants turn up with bags of groceries and the celebrity chefs have twenty minutes to turn it into a meal. The culinary results are always stunning and it never ceases to amaze me what they can do with a few meagre ingredients. But if you think that's impressive, have a listen to what Jesus did one day:

Jesus had been busy and had wanted to get away from the crowds by relaxing by the side of a lake in Galilee. Most of his work took place in this region and he had obviously already earned quite an amazing reputation. Not surprisingly, he was followed by massive crowds who brought to him the lame, the blind, the crippled, those who couldn't speak and many others. He healed them, but was concerned that there were so many there who had been following him for up to three days and had not been able to eat anything.

Mobile catering vans were still to be invented, so all his disciples could find were five small barley loaves and two tiny fish, which would have been plentiful in Lake Galilee and probably only sardine-sized! This was not a major obstacle for Jesus, though, so he took them, looked up to heaven, thanked God and then passed them around. The Bible records that all the people ate and were satisfied, that twelve basket-fulls of leftovers were collected, and that 5,000 men had been fed, not counting women and children. Wow!

He raised the dead

On three different occasions Jesus brought people back from the dead. One day in a small town called Nain, some ten miles south-east of Nazareth, Jesus stood and watched a funeral procession. It was a heartbreaking sight, a devastated widow, her husband already deceased and now her only son dead too. The coffin, not like our modern coffins, was probably just a board on which the body laid. The mourning cortege passed by and Jesus stopped it. He told the boy's mother to stop crying, and told the corpse to get up. The young man sat up immediately and began to talk. (Luke 7:11-15).

He claimed to be God

In 1936, a radio broadcast was transmitted to America from England. Just before the voice of King Edward VIII was to be heard, someone tripped over a wire in the control room at the radio station and snapped the only line of communication between the two countries. The engineers were frantic. With only a few moments remaining before air time a quick-thinking apprentice grasped the two broken ends of the wire and bridged the gap. Seconds later the King addressed the nation. In a very real sense, his words were being transmitted through the body of that man.

That's the essence of Christianity. Christians believe that Jesus was God in human form—that Jesus was God in a body. He didn't come to stop suffering, he came to suffer with us, he came to experience every emotion that we feel; laughter, hope, pain, despair. God entered our time, space world to experience it first-hand for himself and to make a difference.

He forgave sin
In the New Testament the Greek word most often used for 'forgiveness' actually means 'sending away' or 'release.' Literally it's the taking away of wrong doing and the guilt that goes with it. Jesus once told a story of a wayward son who rebelled against his father (Luke 15—The Prodigal Son), but who was received back with open arms and forgiveness. I'm sure we all know from personal experience, that forgiveness isn't always an easy thing, and in many ways it has a real cost to it. Christians believe that through Jesus' death and resurrection he made God's forgiveness possible for our wrong thoughts, words and actions. In other words, God's forgiveness cost God the life of his one and only son.

These eight recorded stories, talks and miracles, that I've mentioned, are just scratching the surface, really. It's fascinating that, in total, only 50 or so days of Jesus' work is touched upon in the combined Gospel accounts. That's not a lot in three years of public travelling, or put another way 1000 days or so. That means less than 5% of the days Jesus was ministering are actually recorded. Just imagine all the conversations, the fun and laughter, and indeed all the other miraculous things we've never even heard about.

It's hardly any wonder, really, that John wrote in his book: "Jesus did many other things as well. If every one of them were written down, I suppose that even the whole world would not have room for the books that would be written." (John 21:25).

SEVEN

Why did Jesus die?

JESUS HAD BEEN TRAVELLING and preaching for around three years now with his radical words and actions. We've looked briefly at just a handful of them. Understandably he had made many friends, but many enemies too—mainly of the religious variety, and they schemed and plotted to kill him. He spoke out against religion and its endless rules and regulations and talked about 'life', indeed abundant life, through knowing God. This new life was for everyone, Jew and Gentile. Jesus was a breath of fresh air and upset the status quo of old religion. They had to get rid of him.

The time was April AD 30 and Jesus' extraordinary life was about to come to an end. Whilst he was in Bethany, the Sannhedrin (the Jewish court) were meeting in the High Priest's palace to arrange for his arrest and execution. Jesus' work was almost over.

He knew his mission was nearing its end, so he wanted to spend his last days with his friends. He arranged a meal, which has become known as The Last Supper, where they sat and ate unleavened bread and drank red wine. Jesus knew that there was a traitor at the table, and that one of his closest friends, one of his very own disciples, was about to betray him—it was now inevitable. After supper, they sang a hymn together and then went to a garden, called Gethsemane, on the west slope of the Mount of Olives to pray.

Gethsemane means 'oil press' and was probably originally an orchard of olive trees surrounded by a wall. It was here that Jesus agonised as he mentally prepared himself for what lay ahead. Whilst he was praying and talking to his friends, Judas his betrayer arrived with a crowd of Temple police carrying swords and clubs. One of the disciples put up a bit of a fight but realising it was futile, fled and left Jesus all alone. He was then led away to his accusers.

Practically every legal rule was broken in an attempt to convict Jesus. Jewish law had banned trials at night, during the festival of Passover, and without witnesses—all of which happened during Jesus' trial. The whole case should have been dismissed; it was a total sham. He was taken initially to the High Priests house. Joseph Caiaphas had been High Priest for eighteen years, and was desperate to find something false against Jesus, particularly some evidence that the Roman Governor would recognise. Many people came and told lies and gave false evidence but the Council could still find no reason to kill him.

He endured three different religious trials and eventually the High Priest charged him with blasphemy, as he claimed to be equal to God. Then the people spat in his face and beat him with their fists.

Having orchestrated the arrest, trial and the false witnesses, the religious Chief Priests still had to ensure that the actual execution took place. For this they needed Roman authority and this is why Jesus was taken to Pilate. So, very early the next morning, the leading priests having already decided that Jesus should die, he was tied and led away to Pilate.

Pontius Pilate was the Roman Governor of Judea between AD 26—37. Cruel and unpopular with the Jews, he was afraid his unpopularity with them would mean the loss of his office. In the case of Jesus, he even tried to shirk the responsibility of a final decision by trying to get Herod, the governor of Galilee, who happened to be in Jerusalem at the time, to take over the case. Between them they had declared Jesus innocent of all the charges brought against him and desperately wanted to release him. He was innocent, but the crowds were not interested in justice, instead only in his death.

Passions and tempers were inflamed, the Jews seemed ready to riot, and, afraid that he would be accused before Caesar, Pilate, a very weak man, sought to extricate himself from the situation, and remove all responsibility from

himself for the final decision about to be made. '...he took some water and washed his hands in front of the crowd. Then he said, "I am not guilty of this man's death. You are the ones who are causing it."' (Matthew 27:24) The death sentence had been passed.

If you are at all squeamish, let me warn you in advance that crucifixion was an extremely violent and bloody death. We seem to have forgotten how cruel and hideous the whole process was. Movies about the life of Jesus never seem to portray his death terribly accurately, because to do so would immediately turn the film into an '18' Certificate because it would have to be so gory to accurately record what actually happened.

Once it had been decided to crucify a person, it was customary for the condemned man to be brutally beaten half to death. The Roman soldiers would have used a whip consisting of long leather strips bound together at one end into a strong handle. Into each of these strips would be sewn sharp pieces of bone and lead to inflict serious damage. Jesus would have been tied to a vertical post and the whip would be lashed against his shoulders, back and legs, the first lashes tearing into the skin, further lashes causing more serious damage.

Eusebius, a third century historian, described the flogging of prisoners with these graphic words, "The sufferer's veins were laid bare, and the very muscles, sinews and bowels of the victim were opened to exposure." The centurion in charge would have stopped the beating when he reckoned the prisoner was near death. It was also customary after the beating to mock the prisoner, and the Bible tells us this is what happened to Jesus. He was forced to wear a purple robe and a crown made out of thorns. He was cursed, spat on and then led to the place where he was to be crucified, to Golgotha, which means 'the place of the Skull.'

His back had been torn to shreds yet he had to carry the wooden crossbeam on which he was to be crucified. When they arrived at the execution site, large nails were banged into his wrists and feet, and the cross was pulled up into position. Death now was only a matter of time.

In many religious books and buildings we see ridiculous images of Jesus hanging upon a cross, smiling, looking as if he'd just had his hair permed. I personally find those images offensive, because it really wasn't like that at all in any shape or form. Crucifixion was a brutal way to kill someone. The Roman statesman, lawyer and scholar, Cicero, called it "the most cruel and hideous of tortures." And it certainly was.

What actually used to kill people, apart from the pain, blood loss, shock and trauma was asphyxia, or as it is more commonly known, suffocation. The human body hanging from the arms had to keep pushing itself up to just breathe, and, remember, nails were knocked through the feet. In the end the pain got just too much and the prisoner suffocated. Incidentally, if the person was taking too long to die the guards would break both legs making it impossible for the prisoner to push himself up. Death followed very quickly indeed. This wasn't necessary in Jesus' case as he was already dead.

Just before he died, he shouted: "It is finished." When we look at the phrase translated back into the original Greek it becomes: 'Tetelestai.' Archaeologists have repeatedly found its Latin equivalent, 'consummatum est,' scrawled against ancient tax receipts, indicating that it had been 'paid in full.' Christians believe Jesus' death made it possible for us to know forgiveness for the wrong that we do, and that Jesus paid the price for these wrong things that separate us from God—literally he wiped the slate clean.

The moment he died, the sun went dark and a curtain was torn in the Temple. The darkening sky was a supernatural occurrence and was a sign to the Romans and the other non-Jews. The tearing of the curtain had a great deal of religious significance for the Jews, as the curtain, which represented separation between God and man, now destroyed. Access to God was made available through Jesus and was now the right of anyone, Jew and non-Jew alike.

Anyway, back to the dead body. Don't forget it was imperative that Jesus was dead; he had openly said that he would come back to life. So one of his executioners thrust a spear into his side and blood and water came out. Blood came from the heart. Doctors have told us that the watery fluid came from the sac surrounding the heart. Therefore, Jesus probably died not from suffocation but of heart failure. Quite literally, he died from a broken heart.

Was Jesus really dead?

THIS IS A VERY IMPORTANT POINT. Jesus was most definitely dead—there was no doubt about it, and the disciples had fled for fear that their own lives would be taken too. Most of them had gone into hiding days before, when Jesus was arrested by the authorities in the Garden of Gethsemane. During Jesus' trial, Peter, the best friend of Jesus, had been spotted by the crowds and denied that he even knew Jesus, on three different occasions.

After Jesus had been crucified the Bible tells us they all ran away and hid with the doors locked. (John 20:19) They were terrified and confused. They had never imagined it would finish like this and when they saw Jesus actually die they were completely devastated.

Meanwhile, back at Golgotha, the dead body was being dealt with in accordance with Jewish burial traditions. Jesus' body would have been removed from

the cross and covered with a sheet, then immediately taken to a private tomb owned by a wealthy supporter. The Jews considered washing of the body very important, so this would have been done once they were inside the tomb, and then the body was covered in spices and a white lined cloth. Everyone then left the tomb and a large stone rolled into place across the front.

Modern engineers have reckoned that this stone, a huge disc shaped boulder, placed in front of the tomb would have weighed between $1\frac{1}{2}$ and 2 tonnes, and would have taken perhaps 20 men to move it once it was in position, in a groove or trench to the front of the tomb. Even Clark Kent's alter-ego Superman would have raised quite a sweat moving it once gravity had done its job and it was in place in its groove.

Whilst all this was going on, the Jewish authorities were in a state of panic because even though Jesus was finally dead, thousands were becoming Christians. To avoid any doubt over his death, a well-trained Roman guard unit was sent to secure the tomb where the body lay.

If this 100 man unit, [called a 'Century' for obvious reasons (!)], wasn't enough security, a seal was set on the stone, to prevent anyone from tampering with the tomb in which his body lay. This seal was in fact a cord that was stretched across the massive stone in front of the tomb, and fastened at each end with clay. Finally the clay was imprinted with the official signet of the Roman governor of the time. Tampering with this official seal held serious consequences, and anyone breaking it would have incurred the full force of the Roman law.

The guards were on full alert and the tomb secured. The dead body was going nowhere.

NINE

Did Jesus come back to life?

WHILST WRITING MY SECOND BOOK, 'Man, Myth or Maybe More?' (Silver Fish) I wrote to a whole host of well-known personalities to ask their opinions on who they thought Jesus was.

One of the most interesting views came from Claire Rayner, the British Agony Aunt, who offered a contribution that she reckoned I wouldn't like. This is what she said, see what you think: 'I find aspects of the worship of Jesus more than a little disturbing. For example, the sadomasochistic nature of the 'Adoration' given to the image of a man bleeding to death while pinned to a cross is a very nasty example of glorification of the sort of human behaviour that is deeply disgusting.'

Claire put in her letter that I would probably find this view 'very offensive,' but in a way I have to totally agree with her. It is rather sick that Christians should worship a man being butchered to death on a cross. We see pictures and stained glass windows in churches the length and breadth of the land. Christians and many others wear crosses around their necks. Could you imagine how weird it might look if people wore miniature sets of gallows around their neck, or electric chair earrings. That would be totally tasteless wouldn't it?

I believe Claire Rayner is absolutely 'spot on' in her comments, except for the rather major fact that Jesus didn't stay dead, and that is the vital point. Jesus came back to life again. You see, the resurrection of Jesus is the cornerstone of Christianity. The Bible even tells us that if Jesus didn't come back to life then us Christians are wasting our time, "And if Christ has not been raised, then your faith has nothing to it." (1 Corinthians 15:17) Because of his resurrection, tragedy turned into triumph.

Let me recap for just a moment on the chain of events

surrounding his death. On the Friday he was dead; there was no doubt about it. He had been brutally crucified, then a Roman soldier stuck a spear into his side, to make sure he was dead. The Bible tells us that blood and water poured out, from his heart. His body was taken down from the cross and placed in a tomb, and the grave was then guarded.

On that first Easter Sunday, the women that approached the tomb couldn't fail to notice that the massive stone covering the tomb had been moved and that the soldiers had fled, an offence so grave it would normally have resulted in the death penalty for these 'deserters'. None of them were punished, though, on this occasion. Indeed it looks as if they were 'paid off' by the authorities to keep their silence. This was quite extraordinary.

The women were puzzled by the whole scene. Suddenly two men in bright shining clothes stood before them. Absolutely terrified, the women fell to the floor, as the men said to them: "Why are you looking among the dead for one who is alive? He is not here; he has been raised." As they were leaving, one of the women, Mary Magdalene, then saw Jesus for herself. At the time she didn't properly recognise him. Instead, she thought it was the caretaker, doing a few odd jobs around the cemetery.

If the whole thing had been some elaborate hoax that had been planned by his friends and disciples, then they had been stupid in making the women the first witnesses on the scene. I know it sounds sexist, but in those days the testimony of women was not valid in a court of law. A small, but, I believe, not insignificant point.

The women couldn't believe their eyes and ran back to tell the disciples the amazing news. John and Peter sprinted to the tomb to see for themselves and in the place where Jesus' body had been, lay the white strips in which his body had been wrapped.

Later that same day, he suddenly appeared to the disciples. He was alive, just as he'd promised. Not surprisingly, they were pretty scared and, indeed, thought they were seeing a ghost. According to one of the accounts we have, he later organised a beach barbecue where he cooked breakfast for them. He let his friends touch him and he actually ate grilled fish in front of them to prove he wasn't some sort of ghostly apparition.

This was just the start, though. For over a month he appeared again to his disciples and others on eleven different occasions. Indeed, at one time he was seen by more than 500 people in one go. This was not mass hysteria, or a hallucination, or wishful thinking. Jesus was most definitely alive.

After a period of forty days, it was now time for Jesus to leave. He had risen from the dead, people had touched him and he had eaten with them, but his time on earth was finished. He was going back to be with his father, so he made a final and miraculous departure and ascended into heaven.

How do you explain the resurrection?

SOME YEARS AGO, Frank Morison, an American journalist started to write a book to show that the resurrection never happened. After considerable research he realised that the resurrection really did happen, and he became a Christian. This is what Morison said in the introduction to his book, 'Who Moved the Stone?': 'This study is in some ways so unusual and provocative that the writer thinks it desirable to state here very briefly how the book came to take its present form. In one sense it could have taken no other, for it is essentially a confession, the inner story of a man who originally set out to write one kind of book and found himself compelled by the sheer force of circumstances to write another.'

When we sit back and think about it logically I've got to admit that the resurrection just seems impossible. But once again, our belief isn't merely based upon faith or some strange religious feeling, but upon solid evidence to support it. The resurrection wasn't a first century legend; it really did happen. Let's take a look at some arguments and suggestions as we try to unravel some explanations for that first Easter weekend:

It was just an hallucination

I'm not going to spend too much time on this particular theory, because not wanting to 'beat around the bush' it's just too daft for words. Without getting too technical again, a hallucination is the experience of seeing an object or event that is not actually present to the human senses. In other words seeing something that isn't really there. I'm sure some people might hallucinate from time to time, but not hundreds in one go. Remember after the resurrection, Jesus appeared to around 550 people, once to 500 in one go. Hallucinations only ever occur to certain individuals at a certain time.

I'm sure you can think of the major flaw in this supposed theory anyway. What happened to the body of Jesus? It was most definitely gone, no-one ever disputed that. This was no hallucination.

The body was stolen

Some sceptics have suggested that someone stole his body—but who would do such a thing? Certainly not the Jews or the Romans. Within a matter of weeks, all of Jerusalem was awash with rumours that Jesus had come back to life. Revolution was in the air on the basis of Jesus being alive. If the authorities had the body then why didn't they produce it to put an end to the rumours once and for all?

It is nigh on impossible to believe the disciples had taken it. They were terrified and were hiding out of the city. And anyway, how on earth did they get past 100 well-trained and disciplined Roman Guards? The guards would have faced the death penalty for losing a living prisoner, let alone a dead one! Why would they lie; what was the point? Remember most of the disciples went on to die for their belief that Jesus had come back to life— why die for a lie?

Maybe he never died

There are those who have a crazy notion that Jesus somehow fainted on the cross, miraculously revived in the tomb and simply passed himself off as having come back from the dead. Don't forget crucifixion was a common punishment; it was a slow and terrible form of death. History books tell us that in one day alone 6,000 men were crucified, so it was something the Romans were very good at. They certainly wouldn't have been sloppy enough to have let Jesus survive, especially as their governor Pontius Pilate had personally ordered his death. Jesus was dead. There was no doubt about it.

Anyway, think about it sensibly for a moment. Jesus had been brutally beaten and put through a Roman

scourging, he had been pinned up on a cross for six hours with nails in his hands and feet. A spear was rammed into his side piercing his heart. His body was taken down and wrapped in yards of cloth soaked with spices and fragrances that would have hardened to around 34 kilograms. Then three days later, he woke up and managed to move a 1´ to 2 tonne stone in front of an airtight tomb, fight his way past the Roman Guard, and then walk miles to appear to his disciples as the conqueror of death. Need I say any more? What a load of nonsense!!

It was just a legend

This was no fairy story. We've already looked in detail at the evidence for this event from Jewish writers, Roman historians and the Bible itself. There's also overwhelming supporting evidence. Just one example to consider is the Garden Tomb that was discovered in 1885. General Gordon and his team were convinced that this was the place where the body of Jesus had lain. There is a traditional tomb inside the wall of the modern Jerusalem, but no certainty attaches to the site. This Garden Tomb, hidden for centuries, was covered with rubbish twenty feet high. When they first cleared the spot, with great caution they gathered all the dust and debris within the tomb and carefully shipped it back home to the Scientific Association of Great Britain. Every part of it was analysed, but there was no trace of human remains. If this was the real tomb of Jesus, then Jesus was the first to be laid there and he was also the last.

It was a Miracle

The final option we have when we try to make sense of the resurrection, is that it really did happen. John Singleton Copley, one of the great minds in British legal history, and three times High Chancellor of England, wrote, "I know pretty well what evidence is, and I tell you, such evidence as that for the resurrection has never broken down yet."

In the early part of the 20th Century, a group of lawyers met in England to discuss the biblical accounts of Jesus' resurrection. They wanted to see if sufficient information was available to make a case that would hold up in an English court of law. When their study was completed, they published the results of their investigations. They concluded that Jesus' resurrection was one of the most well-established facts of history!

Of course we can never prove scientifically that the resurrection happened, but we can most definitely prove the facts of history. When you logically think through the possible alternatives that have been offered, you can see major flaws in all their arguments. There's only one real alternative left, and that is that it actually happened as the Bible suggested. It was a miracle, because if God is God then why shouldn't he be able to do it? And the reason he did it, was so that we could know him.

What about Creation and Evolution?

AMERICAN AUTHOR, Charles Swindoll, told in his book, 'Growing Deep in the Christian Life,' how we got cars: 'Many centuries ago, all this iron, glass, rubber, fabric, leather and wires came up out of the ground. Furthermore, each substance fashioned itself into various shapes and sizes. Holes evolved in just the right places, and the upholstery began to weave itself together. After a while threads appeared on bolts and nuts, and amazing as it might sound, each bolt found nuts with matching threads. And gradually, everything sort of screwed up tightly in place. A little later, correctly shaped glass glued itself in the right places. And you see those tyres? They became round over the years. And they found themselves the right sized metal wheels. And they sort of popped on. They also filled themselves with air somehow. And the thing began to roll down the street.

'And one day, many, many years ago—centuries, really—some people were walking along and they found this vehicle sitting under a tree. And one of them looked at it and thought, "How amazing! I think we should call it 'automobile.'" But there's more! These little automobiles have an amazing way of multiplying themselves year after year, even changing ever so slightly to meet the demands of the public.'

We often seem to forget that the 'theory of evolution' is just that—a theory. Indeed, it is less of a scientific theory and more a philosophy about the origins of life and the meaning of mankind. But let me start off by making a distinction between micro and macro evolution. To me, micro-evolution makes sense, and basically means a variation and development within a species. For example, fish, who live at the bottom of dirty

lakes all their lives may lose the use of their sight completely over a period of millions of years. Macro-evolution, however, is completely different, and it means evolution from one species to another—the most famous example being orang-utans becoming human beings like you and me. To me that seems bananas! Something I'm sure the said orang-utans would appreciate! As such macro-evolution is clearly contradictory to the Bible's account of creation.

The opening few verses of the Bible describe it like this: "In the beginning God created the sky and the earth. The earth was empty and had no form. Darkness covered the ocean, and God's Spirit was moving over the water. Then God said: "Let there be light," and there was light.' (Genesis 1:1-3)

Christians, as well as Jews and Muslims, believe that God created the Universe out of nothing, which seems very much at odds with the theory of evolution. But this theory isn't just at odds with the Bible; it also contradicts some very basic laws of science.

Scientists tell us about the second law of thermodynamics, a law of physics, which simply says that left to itself, everything tends to become less ordered, not more ordered or 'complex.' It's a pretty obvious law really, even to a non-scientist like myself: things grow old, run down, decay and eventually die. Batteries run out, your clothes get worn and faded, your trainers fall to bits, gadgets break—ultimately, everything falls apart—things do not get more complex or advanced, as the theory of evolution would suggest.

Always remember, evolution is not a fact. We are often under the impression that Christians are the only one's who don't believe in evolution. I can tell you that dozens of reputable scientists don't believe in evolution either. Professor Wickramasinghe, the astronomer, said this: "The idea that life was put together by random shuffling of constituent molecules can be shown to be as ridiculous and improbable as the proposition that a tornado blowing through a junk yard may assemble a Boeing 747. The aircraft had a creator and so might life."

The Atheist Professor, Richard Dawkins, prefers to call living things 'designoid' to avoid the word 'designed.' But scientists are discovering that the vast universe is so complex that it is ever more logical to believe in a Designer. The great Albert Einstein actually said this: "Everyone who is seriously involved in the pursuit of science becomes convinced that a Spirit is manifested in the laws of the universe, a Spirit vastly superior to that of a man." Years before that, Sir James Hopwood Jeans, the English physicist and mathematician, stated: "The universe seems to have been designed by a pure mathematician."

The point is this: if God is God, than he would have no problem at all in creating the world exactly as is written in the Bible (Genesis 1—3). Many years ago, the famous scientist Sir Isaac Newton, had an exact replica of the solar system made in miniature. At its centre was a large golden ball representing the sun, and revolving around it were small spheres attached at the ends by rods of varying lengths. They represented Mercury, Venus, Earth, Mars and all the other planets. These were all geared together by cogs and belts to make them move around the sun in perfect harmony.

One day as Newton was studying the model, a friend who did not believe in the biblical account of creation, stopped by for a visit. Marvelling at the device and watching as the scientist made the heavenly bodies move on their own orbits, the man exclaimed: "My, Newton, what an exquisite thing! Who made it for you?" Without even looking up, Sir Isaac replied: "Nobody." "Nobody?" replied his friend, puzzled. "That's right! I said nobody! All of these balls, cogs, belts and gears just happened to come together, and wonder of wonders, by chance they began revolving in their set orbits with perfect timing."

His friends soon got the message! It was plain stupid to suppose that the model just happened. But I think it is even more stupid to accept that the earth and the vast universe came into being by just chance. Isn't it more sensible and logical to accept what the Bible says, "In the beginning, God created the sky and the earth." (Genesis 1:1)

Do you believe the earth was created in just six days?

T HE WORLD WE INHABIT must have had an origin; that origin must have consisted in a cause; that cause must have been intelligent; that intelligence must have been supreme; and that supreme, which always was and is supreme, we know by the name of God." Impressive words from the Russian statesman, Nikita Ivanovich Panin who died in 1783.

The Biblical account in Genesis talks of God creating the earth in six days, and then resting on the seventh. As I've said before, if God is God then surely he would have no problem with creating earth, sky, water, trees, vegetation, wild animals, stars, the sun and people with a click of his fingers, let alone taking a whole week to do it. But how does this tie in with the scientific view that the earth is millions of years old?

My personal view is that the six days recorded in the book of Genesis, weren't literally solar (ie. twenty-four

hour) days as we now know them. The main reason for this thinking is taken from the Genesis account of creation: 'So God made the two large lights. He made the brighter one to rule the day and the smaller light to rule the night. He also made the stars. God put all these in the sky to shine on the earth, to rule over day and over the night, and to separate the light from the darkness. God saw all these things were good. Evening passed, and morning came. This was the fourth day.' (Genesis 1:16-19)

As the sun, one of the 'large lights,' isn't recorded as being created until the fourth day, then 'solar days' couldn't exist for the first three days. Maybe those 'days' were instead periods of millions of years. Another reason for this view is the use of the Hebrew word 'Yom' for 'day.' The word is used in other places in the Bible to indicate longer periods of time than twenty-four hours. In Psalms we see: 'To you, a thousand years is like the passing of a day, or like a few hours in the night.' (Psalm 90:4) or elsewhere: "...to the Lord one day is as a thousand years, and a thousand years is as one day." (2 Peter 3:8)

As I said at the beginning of this answer, there are those who would disagree with this view, and hold to the literal account. I have to say, as someone who has limited understanding on this specific subject, there is no compelling reason to throw either theory out. Either way, I believe that God, not some Big Bang or cosmic explosion, was the instigator of earth, the universe and life, and that he created it all so that we as human beings could know him in a personal way.

Christians believe that God put the planets into space with tremendous precision. Our earth is just the right distance from the sun, any closer and we'd burn to a crisp, further away and we'd freeze to death. Scientists also tell us that if the physical properties of the entire universe were minutely different, it would be impossible for us to even exist.

Even Charles Darwin, who wrote the epic book, 'The Origin of the Species by means of Natural Selection' said: "In my most extreme fluctuations I have never been an Atheist in the sense of denying the existence of a God."

Where do Dinosaurs fit into the creation story?

'JURASSIC PARK' AND ITS SEQUEL 'The Lost World', were two of the biggest movies of the late 1990's, and put dinosaurs firmly back on the map, so to speak. Dinosaurs aren't mentioned at all in the Bible, but neither are rabbits, hamsters, guinea pigs and loads of others!

Genesis 1 records that God created 'large sea animals, and everything else that moved in the sea...He also made every bird that flies...He also made wild animals, the tame animals, and all the crawling animals to produce more of its own kind.' The Bible does talk of cattle, oxen, goats and sheep, who were important to the economy of the day. Plus it lists other specific animals, clean and unclean, but Veloceraptors and Tyrannosaurs don't even get a look in, although the Bible does talk about the 'Leviathan' and 'Behemoth', large creatures who inhabited the earth.

It seems pretty obvious, from all the fossil remains, that dinosaurs did most definitely exist; the records we have in museums across the world make for compelling evidence. What is interesting is that these exhibits are of a particularly well-preserved nature, with often complete skeletons intact. A catastrophe, such as a world-wide flood would explain having such excellent remains.

Such a flood did occur according to Genesis. After the 'fall,' the moment in history where Adam and Eve rebelled against God and his plan for perfect friendship and relationship, things went very badly wrong.

So bad that God destroyed everyone and everything on the face of his earth. Everything except Noah's family and two of every kind of living creature, which he caused to come to Noah for safekeeping on his ark. It's just possible that God didn't cause Dinosaurs to come to

Noah. Maybe he intended for them to become extinct at that time, or maybe because of the change in climate after the flood they just died out. We'll never really know.

Hasn't science disproved God?

$$15^2 \times ab3 \div 7x$$
$$19^7$$
$$ab^2$$

I
T IS SCIENTIFICALLY IMPOSSIBLE to prove the existence of God, though I might add, it is scientifically impossible to disprove it too. You can't just put God in a test-tube and analyse him in a laboratory. So sorry, I'm afraid there isn't any concrete proof that God lives.

Having said that, the Bible tells us that God exists. Christians believe that the Bible is much more than just a book, they believe that it is the actual word of God. Christians also believe that God exists because of Jesus, who was God in human form. The Bible says: 'The Word became human and lived amongst us.' (John 1:14). The author goes on to tell us that, '...he (Jesus) has shown us what God is like.' (John 1:18)

We can look at our world, and human beings, animals, trees and the weather. Surely it couldn't have all happened by accident? Our world bears all the hallmarks of a creator. The human body, for instance, is a masterpiece of incredible design. Beautifully engineered, it is governed by several hundred systems of control—each interacting with and affecting the other. The brain has 10 billion nerve cells to record what a person sees and hears. The skin has more than 2 million tiny sweat glands—about 3,000 per square inch, all part of the intricate system that keeps the body at an even temperature. A 'pump' in the chest makes the blood travel 168 million miles a day—that's the equivalent of 6,720 times around the world! The lining of the stomach contains 35 million glands secreting juices that aid the process of digestion. And these are just a handful of the incredibly involved processes and chemical wonders that operate just to sustain life.

Science and Scripture do not automatically cancel each other out. They simply look at the world from different perspectives, which doesn't mean they necessarily contradict each other. Professor Albert Einstein said this: "A legitimate conflict between science and religion cannot exist. Science without religion is lame, religion without science is blind."

Science can never prove that God is irrelevant to the universe. If God created it and set it up, as millions of Christians believe, then he is certainly most relevant! Science has never stopped belief in God, and many great scientists including Einstein, Edison, Newton, Boyle, Faraday, Pasteur, Kepler and Copernicus believed in God. Eighty years ago a survey of scientists revealed that 40% believed in God. You might think with all the scientific breakthroughs and discoveries since that time, this figure might have changed quite drastically. But an identically worded survey recently published by the journal, Nature, arrived at an almost identical result—

four out of ten scientists believe in God.

An article in the journal 'Science' in 1997 declared: 'Recent signs point towards a thaw in the ice between science and faith'. Then in the summer of the following year the respected magazine 'Newsweek' in its cover story proclaimed: 'Science Finds God.' Back in the UK, one modern British organisation, Christians in Science, has members and contacts numbering some 1500 scientists, including university staff, scientists in industry and science teachers.

Remember, science asks "how" questions, Christianity asks "why." The crux of the matter is this: the Bible isn't intended to be a science book; instead it's a book about a loving God who created people to have a friendship with them. Adam and Eve mucked it up in Genesis, so God sent Jesus to make things right, so that we could know him again...if we want.

Why is the Bible so important?

"**B**ORN IN THE EAST and clothed in Oriental form and imagery, the Bible walks the way of all the world with familiar feet and enters land after land to find its own everywhere. It has learned to speak in hundreds of languages to the very heart of man. It comes into the palace to tell the monarch that he is a servant of the Most High, and into the cottage to assure the peasant that he is a son of God. Children listen to its stories with wonder and delight, and wise men ponder them as parables of life." Henry Van Dyke (1852-1933), American writer, poet and essayist.

The Bible is astonishing. It has been banned, burned and beloved. It has been read by more people than any other book in the history of the world. It is presented to kings and queens at coronations, to presidents when they are sworn in, and to witnesses in courts of law. It has been more attacked than any other book in history, with generations attempting to discredit it. It has been carried into prison cells, and smuggled into countries where it is outlawed by evil dictators, yet I would wager it gathers more dust on more shelves than any other book. It is certainly a remarkable book.

We have the English Bible because of scholars like John Wycliffe and William Tyndale. Tyndale, for example, finally finished translating the Bible into English in July 1525 and throughout his life faced intense opposition for doing so. His life would have made even a James Bond movie seemed dull, as he faced narrow escapes and numerous action-packed adventures along the way. But on 16 October 1536, he was finally caught and strangled to death. Then, for good measure, his captors burned his body at the stake. His enemies must have thought that was the end of Tyndale and his Bible, but they were so

wrong. The product of his labours, the English Bible is with us today—a book that William Tyndale certainly thought was well worth dying for.

I don't suppose many people walking into a book store whilst shopping on a Saturday afternoon, and asking for the world's best-selling book would expect to be sold the Bible! But it is true. The Bible is the world's number one best-seller, and is quite an amazing book. The Bible or portions of it have been published in 1,783 languages and dialects. The United Bible Societies of America and Europe now distribute 500,000,000 Bibles a year, which are now available in the languages of 97% of the world's people.

Mahatma Gandhi said:

"You Christians have in your keeping a document with enough dynamite in it to blow the whole of civilisation to bits; to turn this world upside down; to bring peace to this worn-torn world. But you read it as if it were just good literature, and nothing else."

A recent archaeological report in the science magazine, "Discovery," contained amazing findings about the Old Testament. Before the discovery of the Dead Sea Scrolls in 1947, the oldest Hebrew manuscript dated about AD 900. The Dead Sea Scrolls, in startling agreement with the Masoretic text, dated to about 150 BC. Yet now archaeologists have discovered a pair of tiny silver scrolls that date back to about 600 BC! While digging at the site of a 5th century church in Jerusalem, researchers found a Roman legionnaires' cemetery. Exploring still deeper, they found a small burial cave containing the scrolls. Very carefully, less than a millimetre at a time, the scrolls were unrolled. On each of them appeared an excerpt from the book of Numbers that included the word, "Jehovah." These scrolls date back to the days before the exile to Babylon, earlier than liberal scholars supposed that the Pentateuch (the Torah) had even been written.

I'm digressing a bit, but my old school history teacher, Mr Pope, would be proud of me! The point I'm trying to make is that the Bible is real and not just exaggerated legends handed down over the centuries. The key evidence for the existence of Jesus is found in the pages of the New Testament, originally written in Greek with most of the books dating between AD50 and AD100. It begins with the four Gospels; called Matthew, Mark, Luke and John, these are the main eyewitness accounts of the life, death and resurrection of Jesus.

The New Testament contains 27 separate books that were all written in the first century AD, less than 70 years after Jesus' death. They contain the story of his life and the beginnings of the Christian church from around 4 BC. The facts were recorded by eyewitnesses, who gave first-hand accounts of what they had seen and heard, "We write to you now about what has always existed, which we have heard, we have seen with our own eyes, we have looked at, and we have touched with our hands. We write to you about the Word that gives life." (1 John 1:1)

Back, to the original question: what's so special about this book? We've already seen that Christians believe that the Bible is the word of God, and although it was written by men and women, they were inspired by God, meaning that ultimately God was the author of the Bible. 'All scripture is given by God and is useful for teaching, for showing people what is wrong in their lives, for correcting faults and for teaching how to live right.' (2 Timothy 3:16)

The actual word 'Bible' comes from the Greek word 'biblia' meaning 'books.' It is made up of 66 books in one, written over a 1,500 year period by over forty authors; fishermen, soldiers, kings, peasants, philosophers and even Daniel, a Prime Minister. The Bible was written in three languages, Hebrew, Aramaic and Greek and includes history books, biographies, poems, songs and even a book of love letters! For all its diversity however, the Bible is a unit. From beginning to end it tells the story of God's plan for friendship with mankind, which people got wrong, and Jesus made right.

Isn't the Bible full of mistakes and contradictions?

SIXTEEN

I OFTEN GET ASKED THIS QUESTION when I'm working in schools. My immediate answer to the questioner is "which errors do you have in mind?" I can honestly say, with my hand on my heart, 99 times out of 100, the person can't think of any. They've heard someone else say that the Bible is full of mistakes, and they've swallowed the misconception hook, line and sinker!

Having said that, I have to admit that sometimes the Bible does appear to contradict itself, though time and time again, apparent contradictions have been explained by archaeological discoveries. Dr. Nelson Glueck, an outstanding Jewish archaeologist, whilst writing his book, 'Rivers in the Desert,' made this remarkable statement: 'No archaeological discovery has ever controverted a biblical reference.' Bear in mind that this incredible statement came from one of the world's leading archaeologists.

Let's take a look at one supposed contradiction. First, let's look at the definition of the word contradiction. It means, 'a statement of the opposite.' For example, if the Bible says (which it doesn't) that Jesus died by strangulation, and that elsewhere Jesus instead died by being crucified, then that would be a contradiction.

Anyway, onto a supposed contradiction, that

concerns the angels who were at the tomb of the crucified Jesus. The four gospel writers seem to report differing accounts. Matthew and Mark relate that one angel spoke to the women, whilst Luke and John state that two angels were at the tomb. At first sight this would appear to be contradictory. However, Matthew and Mark didn't say there was only one angel at the tomb, but instead that one angel spoke to the women. You see the difference?

It's a little like the other week when I popped down to the Rustington Sports and Social Club with my mates Simon and Scott. We had a couple of pints and had a chat with my other friends Arthur and Chris. Someone mentioned to my wife that they'd seen me and Scott going into the club with Simon, then someone else mentioned that they'd seen me having an in-depth conversation and a bag of cashew nuts with Arthur. Now of course both of these witnesses were telling the truth, but these two accounts of my Sunday night out look completely different. They just came from different witnesses from different perspectives. Both statements however are completely true.

Anyway, back to the Biblical account. Although some of the details are different, which you would expect from different eyewitnesses, they agree on the important key points that Jesus was dead, buried and rose again. Wilbur Smith, a respected scholar, had this to say about the differences in the resurrection accounts:

'In these fundamental truths, there are absolutely no contradictions. The so-called variations in the narratives are only the details which were most vividly impressed on one mind or another of the witnesses of our Lord's resurrection, or on the mind of the writers of these four respective Gospels.

'The closest, most critical, examination of these narratives throughout the ages never has destroyed and can never destroy their powerful testimony to the truth that Christ did rise from the dead on the third day, and was seen by many.'

Hasn't the Bible been exaggerated over the years?

THE EMINENT SCHOLAR, F.F. BRUCE, was clearly impressed by the Bible. This is what he observed, "The Bible, at first sight, appears to be a collection of literature—mainly Jewish. If we enquire into the circumstances under which the various Biblical documents were written, we find that they were written at intervals over a space of nearly 1,400 years. The writers wrote in various lands, from Italy in the west to Mesopotamia and possibly Persia in the east. The writers themselves were a heterogeneous (I had to look this up! It means 'diverse in character') number of people, not only separated from each other by hundreds of years and hundreds of miles, but belonging to the most diverse walks of life. In their ranks we have kings, herdsmen, soldiers, legislators, fishermen, statesmen, courtiers, priests and prophets, a tent-making Rabbi and a Gentile physician, not to speak of others of whom we know nothing apart from the writings they have left us. The writings themselves belong to a great variety of literary types. They include history, law (civil, criminal, ethical, ritual, sanitary), allegory, biography, personal correspondence, personal memoirs and diaries.

Bruce continues, "For all that, the Bible is not simply an anthology; there is a unity which binds the whole together. An anthology is compiled by an anthologist, but no anthologist compiled the Bible."

There are important words from someone who really 'knows their onions' so to speak! It just goes to show the Bible is unique. Let's take a look at how it was written. The Jews preserved the manuscript like no other manuscript had ever been preserved. The original biblical manuscripts would have been written onto papyrus, parchments, vellum (calf skin), stone, clay and wax tablets, with pointed reed pens or chisels. The manuscripts were then copied with meticulous care and accuracy. The Jews had special groups of men whose sole duty was to preserve and reproduce the original manuscripts. They took their job very seriously, and even the tiniest and most insignificant error would mean the whole manuscript would be destroyed and they would have to start over again.

The New Testament soon became the most frequently copied and widely circulated book of the ancient world. There are currently 24,633 manuscript copies or portions of the New Testament in existence today, compared with just 10 and 7 copies for Julius Caesar and Plato respectively. You can see what a huge difference that is. Author John Robinson wrote, "The wealth of manuscripts, and above all the narrow interval and time between the writing and the earliest extant copies, make it by far the best attested text of any ancient writing in the world."

As for the Old Testament, another scholar Robert Wilson confirms its trustworthiness too. He mentions the Biblical accounts of the forty kings living from 2000 BC to 400 BC. Each appears in chronological order "...with reference to the kings of the same country and with respect to the kings of other countries...no stronger evidence for the substantial accuracy of the Old Testament records could possibly be imagined, than this collection of kings." Mathematically, it is one chance in 750,000,000,000,000,000,000,000 that this accuracy is mere coincidence. That's pretty tall odds!

There is so much more that can be said about the trustworthiness of the Bible. I've not even mentioned the supporting evidence of non-Biblical authors or the vast amount of Archaeological evidence. Please refer to the Bibliography at the end of the book if you want to do some further study for yourself. Suffice to say the Bible is completely and utterly trustworthy and historically true.

In spite of all this, the Bible has always been given a hard time. In 1874, for example, the Bible was under particularly severe attack by its critics, so John W. Haley published a defence entitled, 'Alleged Discrepancies of the Bible.' At the end of his introduction he wrote, "Finally, let it be remembered that the Bible is neither dependent upon nor affected by the success or failure of my book. Whatever may become of the latter, whatever may be the verdict passed upon it by an intelligent public, the Bible will stand. In the ages yet to be, when its present assailants and defenders are mouldering in the dust, and when our very names are forgotten, God's word will be, as it has been during the centuries past, the guide and solace of millions."

I couldn't have said it better myself!

What about suffering?

WHAT A TOUGH BUT VERY LOGICAL QUESTION. A friend of mine lost his baby through a tragic cot death a few years ago. He telephoned me in tears, asking: "Why?" I couldn't give an answer; all I could do was pray and be a friend. There seemed to be nothing to say.

Surely if God is as great, loving and caring as Christians make out, why did their baby boy die, and why do so many innocent people suffer so much? The whole suffering question is so hard to answer, and sometimes even impossible. But let me try to give a few of my perspectives on this very hard subject.

Firstly, I'd say if we're really honest, we have to take the blame ourselves for most of the suffering in our world. Whenever a child is abused, a senior citizen mugged, a person murdered you have to point the finger at a human culprit, not God. The Scientist Albert Einstein blamed mankind for the evil in the world, "Evil is a problem in the hearts and minds of men. It is not a problem of physics but of ethics. It is easier to denature (change the properties of) plutonium than to denature the evil spirit of man."

Even natural disasters seem to be on the increase, as the world seems quite literally to be falling apart. Yet God planned it to be so different. In the beginning he wanted mankind to live in friendship with him. Hardship, disease and suffering were not on his agenda.

I remember vividly in my teens watching the BBC report from the famine in Ethiopia in 1985, and Bob Geldof's comments as he stood and witnessed for himself the devastation and said: "Don't blame God, blame man." For only 200 miles away, in the capital Addis Ababa, vast amounts of money were being spent on renovating homes for senior government officials.

More recently, when Hurricane Mitch devastated Nicaragua and Honduras, those unfortunate countries received around $5,000 a day from the west for Hurricane relief, yet had to pay back that very same figure, almost to the cent, in debt repayments. The suffering adults and children were no better off.

On a daily basis, it seems, we turn on our televisions and see people killed in earthquakes and tornadoes and other horrendous natural disasters. As I sit here and write, an earthquake that lasted just 45 seconds hit Turkey, killing 45,000 men, women, boys and girls. It does seem, though, that the devastation that followed the earthquake is not being seen in Turkey as an act of God or a natural disaster. The survivors are blaming the Turkish Government and they, in turn, are blaming dishonest developers who flaunted building regulations, cut corners and turned buildings into death-traps.

Ted Piedenbrock, an earthquake expert and structural engineer, sifted through the rubble in Turkey to find concrete that had been made with too much water, and also mixed with sea shells. A deadly shortcut made to increase the profits of cowboy builders that even the Turkish authorities labelled as "murderers." Piedenbrock told the BBC: "It is not very difficult or expensive to design structures that withstand virtually any size of earthquake with the minimisation of loss of life. The problem is allowing 'cowboy' contractors to continue building." This natural disaster was instead a man-made disaster.

But what of natural disasters that seem to occur so regularly and bring such pain and hardship? We can read in the book of Genesis how God gave people free will to love him, yet they chose to go their own way, and do their own thing. The world seemed to go wrong from that moment on. Christians call it the 'fall,' scientists call it 'entropy' (from the second law of thermodynamics I mentioned earlier). Put simply, the world is in a state of decay and that's why earthquakes, typhoons, cyclones, whirlwinds, erupting volcanoes and the like cause so much damage today.

I have to say though that God is not detached from suffering, or indifferent to it. God tried to rectify the 'fall' by sending his one and only son, Jesus, into the world to try to turn things around. A piece called The Long Silence explains it like this:

'Billions of people were scattered on a great plain before God's throne. Some of the groups near the front talked heatedly—not with cringing shame, but with belligerence: "How can God judge us?" said one. "What does he know about suffering?" snapped a young brunette. She jerked back a sleeve to reveal a tattooed number from a Nazi concentration camp:"We endured terror, beatings, torture and death."

In another group, a black man lowered his collar. "What about this?" he demanded, showing an ugly rope burn. "Lynched for no crime but being black! We have suffocated in slave ships, been wrenched from loved ones, toiled till death gave release."

Far out across the plain were hundreds of such groups. Each had a complaint against God for the evil and suffering he permitted in his world. How lucky God was to live in heaven where there was no weeping, no fear, no hunger, no hatred.

Indeed, what did God know about what man had been forced to endure in this world? "After all, God leads a pretty sheltered life," they said. So each group sent out a leader, chosen because he had suffered the most. There was a Jew, a black person, an untouchable from India, an illegitimate person, a victim of Hiroshima and one from a Siberian slave camp.

In the centre of the plain, they consulted with each other. At last they were ready to present their case. It was rather simple: before God would be qualified to be their judge, he first must endure what they had endured. Their decision was that God should be sentenced to live on earth—as a man. But because he was God, they set certain safeguards to be sure he could not use any of his divine powers to help himself.

Let him be born a Jew. Let the legitimacy of his birth be doubted, so that none would know who his father was. Let him champion a cause so just, but so radical, that it brings down upon him the hate, condemnation and efforts of every major traditional and established religious authority to eliminate him.

Let him try to describe what no other man has ever seen, tasted, heard or smelled—let him try to communicate God to men. Let him be betrayed by his closest friends. Let him be indicted on false charges, tried before a prejudiced jury and convicted by a cowardly judge.

Let him see what it is to be terribly alone and completely abandoned by every living thing. Let him be tortured and let him die. Let him die the most humiliating death—with common thieves.

As each leader announced his portion of the sentence, loud murmurs of approval went up among the throngs of people. But when the last had finished pronouncing sentence, there was a long silence. No one uttered a word. No one moved. For suddenly all knew: God had already served his sentence.'

That really is quite something. God has experienced suffering himself, and I believe this can help us through life's problems and difficulties.

One night a man had a dream. He dreamed he was walking along the beach with God and across the sky flashed scenes from his life. For each scene, he noticed two sets of footprints in the sand; one belonging to him and the other to God. When the last scene of his life flashed before him, he looked back at the footprints in the sand. He noticed that many times along the path of his life there was only one set of footprints. He also noticed that it happened at the very lowest and saddest times in his life. This really bothered him and he questioned God about it: "Lord, you said that once I decided to follow you, you'd walk with me all the way. But I have noticed that during the most troublesome times in my life, there is only one set of footprints. I don't understand why when I needed you most, you would leave me?"

God replied: "My precious, precious child, I love you and would never leave you. During those times of trial and suffering, when you see only one set of footprints, it was then that I carried you."

That story, called Footprints, is a wonderful encouragement. God is there for us in the good times and the bad times, because he loves and wants the best for us. He wants that wrong relationship at the 'fall' put right, which is possible because of what Jesus achieved through his death and resurrection.

NINETEEN

Why doesn't God wipe out all evil?

IF THERE IS A GOD then why is there such evil in our world? Why isn't God doing something about it? Surely he could eradicate all evil if he wanted? Many people assume that because evil exists it disproves the existence of God, and to me that seems a pretty fair assumption on the face of it.

I do wonder, though, if God were to wipe out all evil from this world with a wave of his hand, how many of us would be left? Even though we may have never murdered anyone, or mugged a helpless pensioner, we all do wrong and evil in one shape or form. But it wasn't always like that.

As we've seen with the previous question, the world was not designed with evil in mind; evil came with the 'fall' and the selfishness of man. Mankind has brought evil upon itself. I suppose God could have created people as robots to automatically obey his rules, and to love him. But, instead he gave them free will to choose for themselves.

I have wondered why God couldn't just stop the actions of evil people, but once again that would affect people's free will and cause a lot of confusion. For example, a baseball bat when used in anger as a weapon would turn into a banana, and a bullet when fired from a gun in an act of aggression would turn into a jelly baby! There is no place in our society for inconsistencies like this. God would be constantly interfering with free will and affecting the very laws of nature. There would be total chaos.

The author Dorothy Sayers explained it like this: 'For whatever reason God chose to make man as he is— limited and suffering and subject to sorrows and death— he had the honesty to take his own medicine. Whatever game he is playing with his creation, he has kept his own rules and played fair. He can exact nothing from man that he has not exacted from himself. He has himself gone through the whole of human experience, from the trivial irritations of family life and the cramping restrictions of hard work and lack of money, to the worst horrors of pain and humiliation, defeat, despair and death. When he was a man, he played the man. He was born in poverty and died in disgrace and thought it well worthwhile.'

The Russian philosopher, Nikolay Aleksandrovich Berdyayev spoke a lot about evil, and God's part in it, and how it could be used for good: "The existence of evil is not so much an obstacle to faith in God as a proof of God's existence, a challenge to turn towards that in which love triumphs over hatred, union over division, and eternal life over death."

I know evil and suffering are never good, but I do firmly believe that good can come out of evil. In 1999, incredible 'evil' came to the Columbine High School in Denver, USA. Thirteen students were gunned down and murdered by two of their fellow students, Eric Harris and Dylan Klebold, members of the 'Trenchcoat Mafia.' Among those who died were four committed Christians. One of the four, Cassie Bernall, died a martyr's death as she made it clear, amongst the blood and carnage, that she firmly believed in Jesus. Seconds later she was shot dead. Another student, Rachel Scott, was a gifted young actress who dreamed of spreading Christianity through drama. At her funeral, the mourners were asked: "Who will carry the torch that Rachel is passing on?" High School students around the packed auditorium stood in tears, hands raised to heaven as if to carry the torch. Seventeen year old Cassie Bernall's memorial service was packed too, and, at its close, 75 people made a decision to follow Jesus, whatever the cost. That day, good came out of evil.

Let me leave this answer with some more wonderful news. Yes, evil is here and now, but it won't be forever. Christians do believe that evil will eventually be destroyed once and for all. The last book of the Bible, Revelation is apocalyptic (prophetic), and recounts a divine revelation to John to show what is going to happen at the end of the world.

Its words bring hope to Christians in a suffering world that seems to be falling to pieces: 'He will wipe away every tear from their eyes, and there will be no more death, sadness, crying or pain, because the old ways are gone. The One who was sitting on the throne said, "Look! I am making everything new!" Then he said: "Write this, because these words are true and can be trusted."' (Revelation 21:4-5)

One day, maybe even quite soon, paradise lost will be paradise regained.

TWENTY

Do miracles still happen?

WE WERE ABSOLUTELY CONVINCED he was going to die, as it was pretty evident that he'd had a major stroke. Jay, Amber and myself watched as he lay on his side in obvious pain and discomfort. Oh sorry, I've not explained properly, we're talking about Hammy the Hamster here!

Two days earlier, Hammy had escaped 'Houdini-like' from his cage and was chased around the house by our cats Bart and Homer. They caught him once, but he evaded capture and we thought he was gone for good. Then 24 hours later we noticed that the cats were paying particular attention to the pile of toys in the girls bedroom, then all of a sudden Hammy's head popped up amongst the teddies. He had been found! He was carefully placed back in the cage and we monitored his progress carefully.

The next day he took a turn for the worse. There really seemed no hope. His adventure had obviously been too much for him and as he lay on his side kicking his little leg, it looked as if he'd had a stroke. I explained this to the children, and suggested praying for him. We held hands, kept our eyes open to see what would happen, and I prayed along the lines that either God would make him better, or he would let him die peacefully straight away. We all said a loud 'amen' together, and watched to see what would happen.

Well, would you believe it?! Within 30 seconds Hammy got up, had a little scratch and started running on his wheel. As I write this some eight months later, I'm pleased to report that Hammy Legg is still very much with us! Now you might think that this is a stupid story, but it really did happen and this daft little episode taught my children an important lesson as they witnessed for themselves a minor miracle.

As we've already seen, the very first verse of the Bible starts with the miraculous: 'In the beginning God created the sky and the earth...' (Genesis 1:1) and the theme of miracles carries on throughout the Bible. There's creation, the flood and the parting of the Red Sea for starters. Then, in the New Testament, Jesus feeds 5,000 people with the contents of a small boy's lunch box, he heals blind men and exorcises evil spirits to name just three incidents.

Understandably, over the years, critics have attempted to explain away some of these peculiar occurrences. For example, some have said, when talking about the thousands of Israelites who actually walked through the parted Red Sea, that there is an area at the north end of the sea called the Bitter Lakes. Between the Bitter Lakes and the Red Sea there was a marshy connection just two to three inches deep. These 'experts' claim a south-east wind blew up the channel holding the water in the Bitter Lakes, while the tide ebbed away in the Red Sea. So the Israelites simply walked through the marshy area.

Now this all sounds fairly plausible really until you

start to look at the major weakness in this explanation. If the people of Israel walked across a shallow marshy area, then how come the well-trained Egyptian army that were pursuing them, drowned in just two inches of water? Now that would have been the miracle!

Just because things sometimes occur outside of our usual experience, reasoning and understanding, doesn't automatically mean that they haven't happened. Let me give you a few examples collected from around the world, not necessarily miracles, but all true stories that perhaps show that the impossible does sometimes become possible:

With a piercing scream, 29-year-old New Yorker, Elvita Adams, flung herself from the Empire State Building's observation tower, on the 89th floor. Seconds later, she was practically back where she had started—plucked from death by a freak up-draught of air. The 30mph gust had whipped her back up the face of the 1,472 feet high skyscraper and dropped her on the 85th floor. Hearing her moans, security guard, Frank Clark, opened the window and pulled her to safety inside. Elvita, who escaped with very minor injuries and bruises said: "I guess the good Lord didn't mean for me to die just yet."

Statisticians have calculated that the chances of getting a complete suit dealt to you in the card game, Bridge, is 158,753,389,999 to 1. But this actually happened to Bill McNall at the Carlton Club in Gateshead in March 1992. He dealt himself a 'hand' consisting of all thirteen hearts!

Mrs Lois Sattler of Sydney, Australia, sat on top of Pulpit Rock in the Blue Mountains admiring the view. A scene from Monty Python's Holy Grail sprang to her mind. She turned to her friend and said, "Wouldn't it be funny if God were to strike this mountain." Hardly were the words out of her mouth, than a bolt of lightning zapped out of a suddenly darkened sky and struck her on the behind, tearing the seat out of her jeans. "It's a good job I'm not religious or I might have thought it was very strange," said Mrs Sattler.

Crazy, aren't they? But they all really did happen. Let me tell you about astonishing miracles happening on a daily basis on the other side of the world. In South America, the New Life Christian Centre in Argentina has grown from 100 people in 1982 to around 4,000 people in 1999. The Church is heavily involved in evangelism and see some 200 people (including many children) respond to God each week.

These children from the church, regularly visit their peers at the Garraham Childrens' Hospital to pray for other child patients there. This hospital visitation has seen staggering results, including AIDS-infected babies being healed. In fact there have been so many miracles happening that the church has its own 'department of miracles' with a doctor working hard to verify the miracles of healing. Absolutely incredible!

In closing, let me say this: miracles can and do still happen today. If we take the miracles from the Bible, then there is no message left. The very heart of Christianity is the miracle of God becoming a man in the body of Jesus, who lived, died and rose again so that we could know real life for ourselves.

TWENTY-ONE

What about other religions?

DON'T ALL ROADS LEAD TO GOD? I've heard that said hundreds of times. It's a bit like saying all roads lead to Rustington! Utter rubbish!! This assumption is that people from different religions are experiencing the same God, yet expressing it in different ways.

I really believe that can't be true. They're all so different, let me give you one example of Jesus' words on the subject of forgiveness: "When you are praying, if you are angry with someone, forgive him so that your father in heaven will also forgive your sins." (Mark 11:25)

Powerful and forgiving words from the founder of Christianity. Now compare that quotation with the words of Moslem leader, Ayatollah Khomeini, on the same subject of forgiveness, when he was talking about the author Salman Rushdie on the publication of his controversial book, The Satanic Verses: "Even if Salman Rushdie repents and becomes the most pious man of all time, it is still incumbent on every Moslem to employ everything he's got to send him to hell." Do you notice the subtle difference?!

I do have to say, though, that most religions do have elements of truth and some excellent moral teaching— many of my best friends are Hindus and they are fantastic people. But we need to look at the words of Jesus again. "'I am the way, and the truth, and the life. The only way to the father is through me'" (John 14:6). You can't really argue with that. Christianity isn't about going to church twenty-five times on a Sunday, or watching Songs of Praise! Christianity is all about a personal relationship with God that is only available through his son, Jesus.

The originator of a new religion came to the great French diplomat and statesman, Charles Maurice de

Talleyrand-Perigord and complained that he was having problems converting people to his new religion. "What would you suggest I do?" he asked. "I should recommend," said Talleyrand, "that you get yourself crucified, and then die, but be sure to rise again on the third day."

You see, Christianity is unique because its founder is still alive. No other religion claims that. You can visit the graves of the founders of all the others. Jesus is the only one who is still alive.

What happens when you die?

A MAN HAD A FRIEND who was expanding his business. Business was indeed booming, so much so that a larger warehouse and sales offices were needed. Even though the move and all its implications were rather stressful and complicated it really was a thing to be celebrated. For this reason, the man decided to send his friend some flowers on the day on the grand reopening. Unfortunately for all concerned, a new girl started work that day at the florists, and the businessman ended up receiving a floral wreath that was intended for a funeral. Attached to it was a card that read: 'My deepest sympathy during this time of sorrow.' When the man called his friend on the phone to wish him well, he was confronted with the error: "Why in the world," said the businessman, "did you send me these sympathy flowers?" The man went immediately to the florists to demand an explanation. The florist met him outside the shop and was obviously upset. "I am so terribly sorry about the mix-up with the flowers," she said, "but I hope you will be understanding. Your situation is not half as bad as the one down at the Crematorium. The people there received your flowers accompanied by a card that said: 'Best wishes in your new location.'

There seem to be only two certainties in any life. One is death and the other one is taxes! I guess we don't like talking about or dealing with either. In fact we prefer never to even think about them at all.

Let's take a look at the subject of death and the afterlife; something that is inevitable for all of us. Once again, what Christians believe about the afterlife, or heaven, whatever you want to call it, can't be proved absolutely. After all, people just don't come back after they've died to report on it.

Many will have heard of near-death experiences that dying people have experienced. These often seem sensational and often contradictory, but maybe there is something in it to. The American singer, Johnny Cash, in his book 'Man in Black', wrote about the death of his brother, Jack, in 1944. Jack was two years older than Johnny and had always been his hero and role model. On Saturday, 12 May 1944, Jack went to work at his workshop, cutting fence posts. Johnny had tried to talk Jack into going to see a movie with him that day, but funds were low and the family needed the money.

Whilst at the workshop, Jack suffered a horrendous injury in an accident involving a large table saw. He was immediately rushed to hospital, but wasn't expected to live through the day. He was in and out of consciousness for about a week, and it became obvious that he was going to die. The family gathered in the hospital room by his bed. Johnny Cash tells the story:

"I remember standing in line to tell him goodbye. He was still unconscious. I bent over his bed and put my cheek against his and said: 'Goodbye, Jack.' That's all I could get out. My mother and daddy were on their knees. At 6.30am he woke up. He opened his eyes and looked around and said: 'Why is everybody crying over me? Mama, don't cry over me. Did you see the river?'

"And she said: 'No, I didn't, Son.' 'Well, I thought I was going toward the fire, but I'm headed in the other direction now. I was going down the river, and there was fire on one side and heaven on the other. I was crying: 'God, I'm supposed to go to heaven. Don't you remember? Don't take me to the fire.' All of a sudden I turned, and now, Mama, can you hear the angels singing?'

"She said, 'No, Son, I can't hear it.' And he squeezed her hand and shook her arm, saying: 'But Mama, you've got to hear it.' Tears started rolling off his cheeks and he said, 'Mama, listen to the angels. I'm going there, Mama.' We listened with astonishment. 'What a beautiful city,' he said. 'And the angels singing. Oh Mama, I wish you could hear the angels singing.' Those were his last words. And he died."

Cash continued in his autobiography, "The memory of Jack's death, his vision of heaven, the effect his life had on the lives of others, and the image of Christ he projected, have been more of an inspiration to me, I suppose, than anything else that has ever come to me through any man."

I said earlier that no-one has ever come back from the dead to tell us what it was like. Well, actually there has been one person who has come back. No prizes for guessing that that person was Jesus, who was executed in AD30. We've already looked in some detail at the circumstances surrounding his death, and the strong evidence for his resurrection. He really did come back to life, not just for a few minutes but for 40 days. To me that seems pretty conclusive evidence that there is life after death.

Life after death might be wishful thinking but Christians believe it to be a firm reality. In a very real sense there seems to be an excitement about what lies ahead. After all, if God created life, then I'm sure that he planned for more than just 70 or 80 years of it on earth. He created 'eternal life' for those who want it.

In closing, a great American preacher called Dwight Lyman Moody, said this some years before his death in 1899: "Someday you will read in the papers that D.L. Moody of East Northfield is dead. Don't you believe a word of it. At that moment I shall be more alive than now. I shall have gone up higher, that is out of this old clay tenement into a house that is immortal; a body that death cannot touch, that sin cannot taint, a body fashioned like unto his glorious body. That which is born of the flesh may die. That which is born of the spirit will live forever."

What do you think about Reincarnation?

TWENTY-THREE

I'VE OFTEN WONDERED why people who believe in reincarnation, never leave their money to themselves! All right, I'm only joking! This is a good and quite topical subject that we need to examine, albeit briefly. Many people, including more and more in Western countries are finding the idea of reincarnation more logical than the Christian idea of heaven. It even became front page news in British newspapers when the English Football Team Coach, Glenn Hoddle, was forced out of his job because of his alleged comments about reincarnation and karma, during January 1999.

Reincarnation is sometimes also called Transmigration or Metempsychosis, and is simply a belief in the rebirth of the human soul in one or more successive existences. These rebirths might be as a human, animal or even as a vegetable! The major religions that hold a belief in reincarnation are the Asian religions, especially Hinduism, Jainism, Buddhism and Sikhism, all of which started in India.

They all hold in common a doctrine of 'karma'—not to be confused with 'korma' (my wife's favourite Indian dish!). Seriously though, 'karma' means 'act,' and it's thought that what you do in this present life will have its effect in the next life. A case of 'cause and effect' if you like.

As a Christian I certainly don't believe in reincarnation, though there obviously is a big bonus in that it seems to offer a number of chances to get things right. Christianity couldn't really be more different. 'Just as everyone must die once and be judged, so Christ was offered as a sacrifice once to take away the sins of the many people.' (Hebrews 9:27-28). With Christianity there is just one life, one death and one judgement.

So maybe reincarnation isn't more logical. Its popularity maybe lies in the fact that it's more attractive. But being more attractive or more popular doesn't make something necessarily right or true. Doing good, making an effort, and being nice are all well and good, but eternal life is a gift from God, not something we have to strive or work for. It's for those who want it. '...he saved us because of his mercy. It was not because of good deeds we did to be right with him. He saved us through the washing that made us new people through the Holy Spirit.' (Titus 3:5)

Death, I believe, isn't the end, nor is it the start of a bewildering series of reincarnations. To the Christian, death isn't a full stop, it's a comma leading onto an exciting new chapter.

TWENTY-FOUR

Do you believe in heaven?

A FEW HOURS BEFORE THE AMERICAN EVANGELIST Dwight L. Moody died, he caught a glimpse of heaven. Awakening from a deep sleep, he said, "Earth recedes, heaven opens before me. If this is death, it is so sweet! There is no valley here. God is calling me, and I must go!" His son who was standing by his bedside said: "No, no father, you are dreaming."

"No," said Moody. "I am not dreaming; I have been within the gates; I have seen the children's faces." A short time elapsed and then he spoke his last words: "This is my triumph; this is my coronation day! It is glorious!"

As I write these chapters on death, the whole subject and the way Christians view death have become very pertinent to me, as a very dear friend died quite suddenly a matter of days ago. I hope you'll forgive me if this answer gets a bit personal, but this subject is very real to me right now as I remember and mourn my dear friend Allan Botting.

In spite of a large age difference, Allan was a great friend of mine, who always believed in what I did. He taught me how to play croquet, tried unsuccessfully to get me interested in Alpine Plants and was a tremendous supporter. I always enjoyed getting his letters, and his spidery writing was always full of such encouragement. He was a wonderful Christian man, who knew where he was going. You see Allan always believed that when he died he would go to heaven to be with his precious Lord Jesus.

Billy Graham once remarked that he had talked to many doctors and nurses who had held the hands of dying people. The evangelist explained: "They say there is as much difference between the death of a Christian and a non-Christian as there is between heaven and hell." You see, Christians certainly believe death is not

the end, and that an afterlife is not simply wishful thinking, but instead a tremendous hope for the future.

Few of us haven't personally been touched by death or bereavement in one shape or form—it can be such a devastating experience. I was very touched by the words of Fiona Castle, who spoke on BBC Radio the day after her husband, entertainer Roy Castle, died so tragically of cancer. She was asked how her Christian faith had affected them as they faced Roy's death together: "Oh, it's been everything," she replied. "It has strengthened such a lot since we've gone through this. I heard someone preaching somewhere once, and he said that problems are growth indicators, and I latched onto that because it's true. You do grow through the difficult times. You sail along through the easy times, but you have to grow, otherwise you crumble in the difficult times. We've learned so much through the problems that we've both said, all the way through, that we wouldn't be without the experience. It's been brilliant. My Christian faith has strengthened. I know with a deep conviction and assurance that God is in control of every part of our lives." That hope kept Fiona going through the dark days following Roy's death, and that faith in God and his perfect plans can keep you going too, through pain and anguish. God really can help and make a difference.

In closing, I heard a story about an old man who everyday would take long walks, talking to God. On these walks, he and God would talk about all kinds of things— about the important times in the old man's life; when he met his wife, the birth of his children, special Christmases and other things. One day while they were out walking for an especially long time, the Lord looked at the old man and said, "We're closer to my house than we are to yours. Why don't you just come home with me?" And that is what he did!

I think that's a wonderful story and in my mind's eye, I can see my friend Allan pottering around, teaching some novice the finer points of croquet, at home in heaven. Even though I, along with his wife Mary, children and grandchildren, miss him so much, the hope that it's not the end makes it a little easier as we all come to terms with the loss. On the 15 July 1999 Allan went home to the Lord Jesus whom he had loved and followed for so many years. It was indeed his coronation day!

What is heaven like?

TWENTY-FIVE

THE IMAGE I'VE OFTEN HAD OF HEAVEN is of thousands of old people, wearing white nightshirts, fluttering their wings whilst sitting on fluffy clouds playing gold harps and singing 'Kum ba Yah.' Over at the entrance a burly bouncer, called St. Peter, sits at the pearly gates of heaven checking names on a register to see if people are allowed in or not.

I don't know how different that is to your view of heaven? Incidentally, the St. Peter idea comes from the words of Jesus, "I will give you the keys of the kingdom of heaven." (Matthew 16:19). Now he didn't physically give him a set of front door keys and appoint him as a heavenly receptionist/doorman. These 'keys' were given to him symbolically as a sign of his spiritual authority. After Jesus returned to heaven, Peter became a tremendous preacher and saw many miracles happen through his work. You could say he opened the doors of heaven to thousands of Jews on the day of Pentecost, then some, years later, to non-Jews—Gentiles. He was also miraculously released from prison with others before he was executed for his faith in Jesus.

What is heaven like? Well, once again we don't really know—heaven is a total mystery to us. His holiness, Pope John Paul II, rejects the idea of heaven as a place, calling it instead, a "state of being." In July 1999, he told pilgrims in St. Peter's Square, Rome, it was "close communion and full intimacy with God". The Pontiff added: "The heaven in which we will find ourselves is neither an abstraction nor a physical place among clouds. It is a blessed community of those who remained faithful to Jesus Christ and are now at one with his glory."

I have to say I find that a bit confusing. I personally believe the Bible teaches that heaven is an 'actual' place. It could be one of the stars. I don't know, none of us knows. The Bible certainly doesn't give an address or a map! Maybe it is a star in a far off galaxy. I do know, because I've been told, that on a clear night you can see over 2,000 stars in the heavens. With a good pair of binoculars about 100 times as many will be visible. With even better and more powerful equipment you can see even more. There are about 30,000 million suns in our galaxy, then there's the ones we don't know about in ours and other galaxies.

Perhaps heaven is on one of these stars; I know God can find some place to put us in. It really doesn't worry me one slightest bit. Christians know that heaven is where Jesus is going to be, and that it's going to be wonderful, because he's there. That's good enough for me.

Will animals go to heaven?

A NEWSPAPER ADVERTISEMENT READ: 'Lost: one dog. Brown hair with several bald spots. Right leg broken due to car accident. Left hip hurt. Right eye missing. Left ear bitten off in a dog fight. Answers to the name 'Lucky'.'!

I don't know whether you're an animal lover or not, or whether you'd want them to be in heaven if the choice was left up to you? Personally, I wouldn't be particularly upset if wasps weren't in heaven. I've always viewed wasps as being the thugs of the animal, or, should I say, insect world. They remind me of football hooligans as they buzz around in their stripy tops, drinking lager, annoying everyone and generally causing aggravation! I wouldn't be too disappointed if they weren't in heaven, or spiders either for that matter.

I've included this question in the book for my children, who were very upset when their pet Guinea Pig, Shaggy, died. The children wanted to know if their deceased furry friend was going to heaven. But I guess the question isn't just asked by small children. Certainly in Britain, people often find it easier to relate and care for animals than they do for other human beings, so the thought of never seeing their pet again is really quite an issue.

I once heard about a visitor at a zoo who noticed a zoo keeper crying quietly over in a corner. The visitor asked another keeper what the man was crying about, and he was told that one of the elephants had died. Touched by this, the visitor then asked: "I assume he must have been particularly fond of that elephant?" And the reply came back: "No, it's not that. What he's crying for is that he's the one who has to dig the grave!"

Seriously though, pets weren't a big part of life in the Bible, so understandably this isn't a matter that is mentioned. In the Old Testament we read that in the new kingdom: 'Wolves will live in peace with lambs, and leopards will lie down to rest with goats. Calves, lions and young bulls will eat together and a little child will lead them. Cows and bears will eat together in peace. Their young will lie down to rest together. Lions will eat hay as oxen do. A baby will be able to play near a cobra's hole, and a child will be able to put his hand into the nest of a poisonous snake.' (Isaiah 11:6-8).

The last book of the Bible, Revelation, talks at length about heaven, but, sorry, doesn't mention pets, though it does talk about animals being there. The book talks about living creatures, like lions, calves, and an eagle. It also talks of a lamb, all living together in peace and harmony.

That's quite a list, and I guess if bears, cows, wolves and eagles are going to be in heaven then why shouldn't Guinea Pigs, Cats, Dogs and Hamsters as well? As we've seen the Bible makes it quite clear that animals are in heaven, but doesn't say either way if animals that have died on earth, like our pets, will go too. I really wouldn't be surprised, though. It would be just like God, who is so wonderful and generous to allow pets into heaven as well. So maybe, just maybe, we'll meet up with Shaggy again one day!

TWENTY-SEVEN

Isn't Christianity just a crutch?

MANY PEOPLE THINK CHRISTIANITY is just a psychological crutch to get sad and weak people through the humdrum of life. So, is it a crutch? Well, the answer has to be "yes" and "no."

Yes, because knowing Jesus helps us through our lives. We all endure hardships and elements of suffering—Jesus is there for us, and I believe can help us through the good times and the bad times. He's there for us. 'God has said, I will never leave you; I will never forget you.' (Hebrews 13:5)

Then no, it's not a crutch, because as we've seen from the previous answers, Christianity isn't just a nice fairy story like Postman Pat or Snow White and the Seven Dwarfs that cheers us up a bit when we're depressed. It's not like drugs or alcohol to perk us up temporarily when we're feeling down. Christianity is true! Jesus lived and was very real. An anonymous author made this striking comparison when comparing Jesus with others:

'Socrates taught for 40 years, Plato for 50, Aristotle for 40, and Jesus for only 3. Yet the influence of Christ's 3-year ministry infinitely transcends the impact left by the combined 130 years of teaching from these men who were amongst the greatest philosophers of all antiquity. Jesus painted no pictures; yet some of the finest paintings of Raphael, Michalengelo and Leonardo de Vinci received their inspiration from him. Jesus wrote no poetry; but Dante, Milton and scores of the world's greatest poets were inspired by him. Jesus composed no music; still Haydn, Handel, Beethoven, Bach and Mendelssohn reached their highest perfection of melody in the hymns, symphonies and oratorios they composed in his praise. Every sphere of human greatness has been enriched by this humble Carpenter from Nazareth.

'His unique contribution to the race of men is salvation of the soul. Philosophy could not accomplish that. Nor art. Nor literature. Nor music. Only Jesus Christ can break the enslaving chains of sin and Satan. He alone can speak peace to the human heart, strengthen the weak, and give life to those who are spiritually dead.'

So the answer to the original question is, I guess, yes and no. But either way, the Christian lifestyle isn't an easy option, but I've discovered that it is the best way to live your life.

Do I have to go to Church?

TWENTY-EIGHT

A COUPLE WOKE UP ONE SUNDAY MORNING and the wife got dressed for Church. It was just about time for the service when she noticed her husband hadn't even got out of bed. Rather perplexed, she asked: "Why aren't you getting ready for Church?" He said: "Cause I don't want to go." She thought he might be ill or something, so she asked, "Why not?" He said, "Well, there's three reasons really. First, everyone is so unfriendly, Secondly, no-one likes me. And thirdly, I just don't want to go." The wife replied: "Well, darling, I have three reasons why you should go. First, most of

the people are friendly. Second, there are one or two people who like you. And third, you're the vicar! So get dressed!"

I guess if I'd been given £1 every time I've been asked the question: "Do I have to go to Church to be a Christian?" I'd be basking on a beach in the Bahamas right now, instead of sitting here typing in overcast, drizzly Rustington. The answer to the $64,000 question is quite simply: "no". You don't have to go to Church to be a Christian. And, for that matter, going to Church doesn't automatically make anyone a Christian either.

Going to Church doesn't make you a Christian any more than going to McDonald's makes you a hamburger! So it's not an automatic thing, but having said that going to a Church and being a part of it is a very important part of your Christian growth. In actual fact, you don't go to Church, you become part of a Church—that's quite an important difference.

People asking the question have often misunderstood what the Church is all about. And I guess that's the fault of myself as well as other Christians, so: sorry! Church isn't about a building, be it brick, stone, wood, glass, with a steeple, or without one. It's not about pews, chairs, dog collars, collection bags or plates, stained glass windows or crucifixes. The word Church actually means 'people of like mind.'

So you don't have to go to Church to be a Christian. But a Christian will want to go, though, to be with other people of like mind. Also it's fantastic to learn more about God, Jesus and the Bible with others who share the same interests. I thoroughly enjoy watching top flight football on TV at home, but there's nothing like standing on the terraces at a real match with thousands of other supporters, even if it is my local team, third division Brighton and Hove Albion FC! In the same way, a real Christian will want to be with other Christians.

So let me finish by asking you a question. Are you a real Christian?

TWENTY-NINE

Won't a good life do?

U NFORTUNATELY, THE BIBLE DOESN'T ALLOW **anyone to earn their way into heaven. Of course it's great to do good, support charity, be nice to** people and generally be kind and considerate. But the Bible makes it clear: whether we like it or not, our good works and deeds, whilst being very admirable, don't actually bring us into a relationship with God. 'It was not because of good deeds we did to be right with him. He saved us through the washing that made us new through the Holy Spirit.' (Titus 3:5)

Let me explain why just being good isn't enough. I guess it's all got to do with definitions. God's standard of 'good' is perfection, and none of us can reach that. Even if we've never murdered anyone, or stolen goods from the supermarket, however good we think we might be, we don't come up to God's standards of perfection. Paul, a church leader in Bible times, when writing to the Christians in Rome, made it crystal clear: '"all have sinned and are not good enough for God's glory."' (Romans 3:23)

Now that's pretty depressing really: there's nothing we can do to get good enough to get to God. Before you stick your head in the oven and turn the gas on, let me give you the good news. Paul carried on his letter, '"and all need to be made right with God by his grace, which is a free gift. They need to be made free from sin through Jesus Christ."' (Romans 3:24)

The television presenter, Anne Diamond, was speaking on television about 'belief', and this is one of the comments she made: "It doesn't matter what you believe, as long as you are sincere." I've got to say, and apologies to you Anne if you're reading this book, but that comment is utter hogwash! Sincerity has nothing to do with it at all. People can be sincerely wrong about things, does that make things right? I'm sure Adolf Hitler, in his own deranged mind, was sincere about wishing to create a master race, and annihilating 6 million Jewish men, women and children in the process. Those devastating results proved that he was most definitely sincerely wrong.

Sincerity and doing good simply aren't enough. That means good and bad people both need Jesus the same— whoever you are, whatever you've done, Jesus is the only way.

Does prayer really work?

A TAXI DRIVER AND A VICAR WERE STANDING in line to get into heaven. The taxi driver approached the gate and St. Peter said: "Welcome. I understand you drove taxi's. Since I'm in charge of housing, I believe I have found the perfect place for you. See that huge mansion over the hilltop? It's yours." The vicar heard all this and began to stand a little taller. He said to himself, if a taxi driver got a place like that, just think what I'll get.

The vicar approached the gate and St. Peter said: "Welcome. I understand you were a vicar. See that shed in the valley? That's where you'll be living." St. Peter had hardly got the words out of his mouth when the irate vicar said: "I don't understand. I was a vicar. I preached and helped teach people about God. Why does the bloke who drove taxis get a mansion and I get a ramshackle old shed?" Sadly, St. Peter responded: "Well, it seems when you preached, people slept. When the taxi driver drove, people prayed."

It's easy to get confused about prayer. Believe me, you don't have to get down on your knees, close your eyes and speak earnestly in archaic language. Prayer is simply about building a relationship with God. You get to know someone by being with them—it's the same with prayer, it's about spending time with God. I personally find it easiest to pray when I'm out driving, all by myself. Now that's a pretty difficult and rather dangerous thing to do whilst on your knees with both eyes closed!

And it's not just a one-way conversation. Christians believe that God loves to answer our prayers. The Bible says this: "Ask, and God will give to you. Search, and you will find. Knock, and the door will open for you. Yes, everyone who asks will receive. Everyone who searches will find. And everyone who knocks will have the door

opened." (Matthew 7:7-8)

Christians believe God can change things through prayer. James, an early Church leader, encourages us to keep praying and not give up with these words: "When a believing person prays, great things happen. Elijah was a human being just like us. He prayed that it would not rain, and it did not rain on that land for three and a half years! Then Elijah prayed again, and the rain came down from the sky, and the land produced crops again." (James 5:16-18). Now that's pretty powerful praying!

I know prayer works because I've seen it answered when God healed my daughter Amber when she was just seven weeks old. Virtually overnight Amber started getting very ill and was taken into hospital for tests. She was so small and had become dehydrated so quickly that it took the doctors 12 hours to put a drip into her. She then underwent a whole series of tests, including numerous blood tests and even a lumbar puncture to try to find out what was wrong with her. Eventually, x-rays were taken of her tiny stomach and a consultant paediatric surgeon from another hospital came to us with the results.

It turned out that part of Amber's bowel was twisted and she needed immediate surgery. We were whisked off by ambulance to a specialist children's hospital in Brighton for the operation. I took Amber downstairs with the nurses for a few final x-rays prior to her surgery and watched as tubes were put down her nose, and into her stomach to take the barium (a special mixture that is opaque to x-rays) to examine the full extent of the problem.

Now whilst all this was going on, Jemma had phoned some of our friends from Church who in turn promised to phone around and get people to pray. Standing in the room with the medical staff, and watching my tiny baby lying on the table with tubes in her, deep down I knew God could intervene in the situation.

But even I was surprised when the consultant and his team of two radiographers told me that there was nothing wrong with her stomach or bowel any more. They took three different sets of x-rays and were shaking their heads in stunned disbelief at the turnaround in her condition. Well, I had to say something, so I announced to everyone in the room, that we had been praying and that God had done a miracle. The consultant left the room, scratching his head, muttering: "I am very surprised."

There's no doubt about it; God does answer prayers, though prayer isn't about twisting God's arm, hoping that he will give us what we want. The well-known evangelist Billy Graham admitted: "The only time my prayers aren't answered are on the golf course!" No, prayer is about relationship building and discovering God's agenda, not ours. Uppermost on that agenda is God's relationship with us, personally.

The brilliant scientist, Sir Isaac Newton, said that he could take his telescope and look millions and millions of miles into space. Then he added: "But when I lay it aside, go into my room, shut the door, and get down on my knees in earnest prayer, I see more of heaven and feel closer to the Lord than if I was assisted by all the telescopes on earth."

Why are Christians so boring?

MANY HAVE THE IDEA that Christians are miserable, boring wimps who go to Church twenty-five times on a Sunday, video religious TV programmes, go to Israel on holiday and have beards—and that's just the women! I do have to admit that many Christians are very boring people. Jesus said: "I came to give life—life in all its fullness." (John 10:10) So, if they're boring as Christians with this exciting new life that Jesus talked of, just think how much more boring they were before they were Christians!

Then, on the other hand, you may have personally known people like my mate Mark, who was the life and soul of the party, the first to arrive, the last to go. Every time you met him he had a glamorous girlfriend on his arm, spent wads of cash on flashy holidays and loved life. Then he became a Christian. Now his favourite activities involve wearing black, playing cheesy folk-music and helping old ladies across the road, even if they don't want to go! Not a lot of fun, is it?!

Trust me, you don't have to be boring or a killjoy to become a Christian. You don't have to wear black all year round, wear sandals (with ankle length socks of course!) in the winter, and grow a beard. Honest! Being a Christian is about Jesus, and trying to be more like him, and he certainly wasn't boring in any shape or form. This anonymous piece sums things up pretty well:

'He was born in an obscure village, the child of a peasant woman. He grew up in yet another village, where he worked in a carpenter's shop until he was thirty. Then for three years he was an itinerant preacher.

He never wrote a book. He never held an office. He never had a family or owned a big house. He didn't go to college. He never travelled more than 200 miles from the place where he was born. He did none of the things one usually associates with greatness. He had no credentials but himself.

He was only thirty-three when the tide of public opinion turned against him. His friends ran away. He was nailed to a cross between two thieves. While he was dying, his executioners gambled for his clothing, the only property he had on earth.

Nineteen centuries have come and gone and today he is the central figure of the human race. All the armies that ever marched, all the navies that ever sailed, all the parliaments that have ever sat, all the kings that ever reigned, put together, have not affected the life of man on this earth as much as that one solitary life.'

Now, some 2,000 years later, more than $1\frac{1}{2}$ billion people follow him, with Christianity growing at more than twice the rate of any other religion. That's not what I would personally call boring, or irrelevant.

What about all the hypocrisy in the Church?

THIRTY-TWO

THE INFAMOUS OUTLAW, JESSE JAMES, killed a man in a bank robbery and shortly afterwards was baptised in the Kearney Baptist Church in the USA. Then he killed another man, a bank cashier, and joined the church choir and taught hymn-singing. Apparently Jesse loved Sundays, but didn't always have the time to attend Church, as Sunday was the day he robbed trains! What an incredible hypocrite.

Another reason many reject Christianity is because of hypocrisy in the Church. Once again, I have to admit that there are some hypocrites in the Church, as there are in all walks of life. A hypocrite is a person who says one thing but does another.

As well as personal hypocrisy, there is also the more complicated form of hypocrisy of evil done throughout history in the name of Christianity; for example, the crusades, the inquisition and the terrible troubles in Northern Ireland. I have to admit that Christian history does have a dark side, but we do not have to admit that those who performed these evil actions were real Christians. To put it bluntly, their actions represent the very antithesis of what Jesus was all about.

Jesus hated all forms of hypocrisy; this is what he said, or should I say shouted at a bunch of religious hypocrites one day: "You are hypocrites! You wash the outside of your cups and dishes, but inside they are full of things you got by cheating others and by pleasing only yourselves. Pharisees, you are blind! First make the inside of the cup clean, and then the outside of the cup can be truly clean." (Matthew 23:25-26). Jesus got very angry about hypocrisy.

As I've said, the church does have its fair share of hypocrites and has done throughout history. But that never invalidates the fact that the Christian message is true. Let me give you a personal example of what I mean by that.

I am a big fan of Indian food, and whenever I travel I always make the effort to sample some local cuisine, and on an annual basis, make an award for my personal 'Indian Restaurant of the Year.' I was delighted to give the 1999 trophy to my local curry house, the 'New Tandoori Nights' in Rustington, and was pleased to feature in newspaper and local radio interviews about the award. I would tell all my friends about the quality of the food, the size of the portions and the friendly service. But could you imagine if I always ate my curries at other restaurants. What a hypocrite, you might say. If I believed all that I'd said about the 'New Tandoori Nights', then I'd always eat my Indian cuisine there and nowhere else. Well, that's probably true (and in fact is, in this case!). Yet my being a hypocrite does not invalidate the claim that

'New Tandoori Nights' is the best. Do you see what I mean?

There are hypocrites everywhere in life and the church is no exception. But don't write them all off. Just because there are a few football hooligans who are bent on violence and destruction, doesn't mean that every football supporter in the world is out for trouble.

No Christians are perfect, they're all imperfect individuals at the end of the day. But that doesn't make them all hypocrites or frauds, it just makes them fallible people who need the help and forgiveness that Jesus offers. After all, if the great inventor Alexander Graham Bell had been arrested for shoplifting, would that make using the telephone wrong? Of course not! I'm pleased to say that Christianity doesn't stand or fall on the way Christians behave, or have behaved throughout history. Christianity stands on the person of Jesus, who was no hypocrite.

THIRTY-THREE

What is a real Christian?

CONTROVERSIAL SINGER-SONGWRITER, **Mark** Morrison, was released from jail in February 1999, after sending someone else to do his community service for a previous offence. Whilst imprisoned, it was widely reported by the media that he had converted to Islam, the Muslim faith, and had changed his name to Abdul Rahman.

"That was b******t," he insisted on his release. "Anyone can phone up a newspaper and tell them anything. I'm just as Christian as my mother made me. I'm just a Christian—well I try to be anyway."

I personally don't think anyone can be 'made' a Christian by their mother, or anyone else for that matter. So what does make a Christian a Christian? I often ask this question myself in schools lessons to get the young people thinking about what a 'real' Christian is. The answers I get are normally pretty similar:

Someone who believes in God
Someone who goes to Church
People who celebrate Christmas
Someone who has been christened or confirmed
Someone who doesn't swear
Someone who keeps the 10 commandments
Vicars and Nuns
Christians read the Bible

It's very interesting what people think. I believe becoming a Christian is the most important thing anyone can ever do with their life, so it's vital to check out what it means to be a real Christian, so no-one gets the wrong idea. You don't have to sign up to any religious organisation, or become a monk or a nun, or give your money away, trust me!

The word itself, 'Christian,' was originally a nickname given to the very first followers of Jesus. It means 'a follower of Jesus.' Let me explain four important things you need to do and understand to become a real follower of Jesus:

God's Plan

In the beginning God made people and planned for them to have a wonderful relationship with him. We can read in the Bible: "Through his power all things were made—things in heaven and on earth, things seen and unseen, all powers, authorities, lords and rulers." (Colossians 1:16) People need to have relationships, and this relationship with God was perfect, for a while anyway.

People's Problem

People mucked up this perfect relationship with God though, by thinking, saying and doing wrong things. We can read in the Old Testament: "We all have wandered away like sheep; each of us has gone his own way. But the Lord has put on him the punishment for all the evil we have done." (Isaiah 53:6)

The Bible calls these wrong things 'sin', and goes onto say that sin stops us having a relationship with God. Originally the word "sin" was the word archers used to describe missing the target. In the same way we've all missed the target God planned for us. Put another way, our sin separated us from God and nothing we could do could bridge that gap.

A famous rabbi was walking with some of his disciples when one of them asked: "Rabbi, when should a man stop sinning and repent?" The rabbi calmly replied: "You should be sure to repent on the last day of your life." "But," protested several of his disciples, "we can never be sure which day will be the last day of our life." The famous rabbi smiled and said: "The answer to that problem is very simple. Repent now."

Jesus' Solution

Jesus, God's own son, embarked on a rescue mission to do something about this broken relationship, and this gulf and separation caused by our wrongdoing. He came to the world to take away the sin that stops us having a relationship with God, through his life, death and resurrection. He gave his life to give us real life through knowing God personally.

A wealthy English family once invited friends to spend some time with them at their beautiful estate. The happy gathering was almost plunged into a terrible tragedy on the first day. When the children were swimming, one of them got into deep water and was drowning. Fortunately, the gardener heard the others screaming and plunged into the pool to rescue the helpless victim. The young man was Winston Churchill. His parents, deeply grateful to the gardener, asked what they could do to reward him. He hesitated, then said: "I wish my son could go to college someday and become a doctor." "We'll pay his way," replied Churchill's parents.

Years later, when Sir Winston was Prime Minister, he was stricken with pneumonia. Greatly concerned, the king summoned the best physician who could be found, to the bedside of the ailing leader. That doctor was Sir Alexander Fleming, the developer of penicillin. He was also the son of that gardener who had saved Winston from drowning as a boy! Later Churchill said, "Rarely, has one man owed his life twice to the same person."

In the same way, we owe our lives to Jesus. The Bible sums it up like this: "God loved the world so much that he gave his one and only Son so that whoever believes in him may not be lost, but have eternal life." (John 3:16)

Our Choice

So, understanding all this, and acknowledging what Jesus did for us, so we could be reconciled with God, we need to ask God to take over our life as we put our trust in him. This is what becoming a Christian is all about.

"You have been saved by grace through believing. You did not save yourselves: it was a gift from God. It was not the result of your own work, so you cannot boast about it." (Ephesians 2:8-9)

When my wife, Jemma, makes me a cup of coffee, I drink it without question. I don't minutely examine it, or test the chemicals to make sure she's not trying to bump me off, so she can get her hands on the insurance money—I trust her, that's what faith is all about. Some may say that Christianity is "blind faith," that's not so; you can only be really sure when you take your first steps towards Jesus. It really is over to you.

It was the assassinated pastor and civil rights leader, Martin Luther King who said: "If a man hasn't discovered something he would die for, he isn't fit to live." Are you prepared and ready to lay down your life and ask God to take over?

THIRTY-FOUR
How do I become a Christian?

ONE OF THE WONDERFUL CHARACTERISTICS that distinguishes Christianity from other religions is that forgiveness and reconciliation with God is only possible through what Jesus has done, and nothing that we can do. There was a story in a newspaper some years ago that illustrates this pretty graphically!

The headline was "Conversion to Hindu Faith is Tortuous." The article went on to state, "A West German businessman has completed his conversion to the Hindu faith by piercing himself through his cheeks with a $1/2$ inch thick, 4 foot long steel rod, and pulling a chariot for 2 miles by ropes attached to his back and chest by steel hooks. Others walk through 20 foot long pits of fire, don shoes with soles made of nails, or hang in the air spread-eagled from hooks embedded in their backs."

Now that's not a bundle of laughs is it??!! I'm so glad that becoming a Christian isn't like that at all. Maybe it's now the time for you to make a commitment to God by becoming a Christian. You obviously need to understand the four key points that I've just explained, and be ready to take it on board. When you've done that the next few stages are as easy as A,B,C.

Admit
You need to admit that you've done wrong; that you have sinned. You might not have ever robbed anyone, or committed murder, or mugged old ladies to steal their gold fillings, but deep down you know that you have gone your own selfish way instead of God's. The Bible uses the word 'repentance'. That means a deep sorrow about your actions and a turning away from all you know to be wrong. In fact, to say sorry and to be sorry.

"All have sinned and are not good enough for God's

glory." (Romans 3:23)

"When people sin, they earn what sin pays—death. But God gives us a free gift—life for ever in Christ Jesus our Lord." (Romans 6:23)

Believe

Next, you need to believe that Jesus' dying on the cross was the ultimate sacrifice, and his death and resurrection made it possible, for us to start a new life. He paid the price for the death our sins deserve.

"God loved the world so much that he gave his one and only Son so that whoever believes in him may not be lost, but have eternal life." (John 3:16)

"Christ himself suffered for sins once. He was not guilty, but he suffered for those who are guilty to bring you to God." (1 Peter 3:18)

Commit

Now it's time for commitment—to commit yourself to living God's way, from this point forward, as a Christian. When you think about it logically, it's stupid to live any other way. God created us, so he knows what's best for us. Remember the advice we often see on all sorts of products we buy in the shops, "for best results follow the maker's instructions." God won't leave us to it, though; he'll help us. If we put God in charge of our lives he promises to live inside us, by his Holy Spirit, which gives us power to change and get to know God.

"But to all who did accept him and believe in him he gave the right to become children of God." (John 1:12)

So that's it—it's as simple, yet as difficult as that. I urge you not to miss the important step. Believing in God, Jesus or going to Church is not enough. You need to take it a stage further by asking God to take over your life. It makes so much sense, but don't put it off.

One night in 1962, in a hotel room in Seattle, USA, the evangelist Billy Graham was sound asleep. Suddenly he woke up with what he later described as 'a burden to pray for Marilyn Monroe,' the movie actress. When the feeling continued the next day, one of Graham's associates tried to reach the actress through her agent. The agent offered no hope for a meeting immediately. "Not now, maybe two weeks from now," he said. Two weeks later, Marilyn Monroe's suicide shocked the world. Two weeks was just too late.

If you're ready to take things a step further, and you really want to be a Christian, or maybe you're not sure whether you are or not, then here's a prayer that should help you. Please don't get all religious though; prayer is simply talking to God, your dad in heaven. Say this prayer seriously, really meaning it, and God will do the rest.

The Prayer
"Dear Father God,

I am really sorry for all my sins, for all the things I've done, said and thought that were wrong. I choose to turn from those things and live my life your way.

I believe that Jesus died on a cross to set me free, so I could know you.

Please come into my life and fill me with your Holy Spirit, so as from today I can start to live my life in a way that pleases Jesus.

Amen."

If you said those words and really meant them, well, congratulations, you are now a Christian. Do you feel any different? You might; you might not. Don't be disappointed if you don't receive some major supernatural experience, complete with blinding lights and voices from heaven! After all the Christian faith is built upon belief, and not necessarily feelings all the time. Just remember the fantastic words of Jesus: "Here I am! I stand at the door and knock. If you hear my voice and open the door, I will come in and eat with you, and you will eat with me." (Revelation 3:20)

What's next?

THIRTY-FIVE

M<small>Y WORK IN SCHOOLS</small>, colleges, universities and out on the road brings me face to face with thousands of people, young and old, each year. Many of those I speak with agree that Christianity really does make a lot of sense, but are often concerned that becoming a Christian involves becoming very serious and boring. Many have the image of a Wally in grey slacks and sandals and a tight-fitting tank top, singing endless hymns and visiting the Holy Land on an annual pilgrimage! Trust me, it hasn't got to be like that at all!!

The Bible talks about a person being "born again" when they become a Christian, it's like starting life all over again, with a fresh, new start. There are some things you need to do; they're not heavy or religious or any of that business, but they will help you as you live your life for Jesus.

Church

When I was a kid, I used to play football in our garden by myself, kicking the ball against the side of our house, and passing it back—it kept me occupied for hours on end. But the best way to play football was on a Saturday afternoon with the rest of the team. Once you've become a Christian you become part of the Church team and also part of a new family of around $1^1/_2$ billion men, women and children across the world. It's good to spend time with your new family—though obviously not all at the same time!

I want to be honest with you and admit that some Church meetings are really boring, and won't help you much at all. But having said that, loads of them are brilliant. Find a Church that's good, with friendly welcoming people that love God, read and study the

Bible in a helpful way, and are passionate about reaching those who aren't Christians and don't yet know Jesus.

Bible

Once again, we've looked at some length into the Bible, so I won't show off with another load of statistics and information! It might seem a strange thing to say, when it comes to actually reading the Bible, but starting at the beginning might not be the best place to start. The Old Testament tells us how God helped and guided people in the past, whilst the New Testament tells us of Jesus' birth and beyond. So as you start to follow Jesus, why not get to know him a little more by reading the 'gospels', Matthew, Mark, Luke and John, four different authors who tell us the life story of Jesus from their perspectives.

Try to get your hands on a modern translation of the Bible, something that is easier for you to understand, and ask some Christians for some tips on how best to start reading and understanding it.

Prayer

A man ran into trouble while flying his small Cessna aeroplane. He radioed the control tower to urgently speak with one of the air traffic controllers, "Pilot to tower," he said, "I'm 300 miles from the airport, six hundred feet above the ground, and I'm out of fuel. I am descending rapidly. Please advise. Over." "Tower to pilot" the controller began: "Repeat after me: "Our Father who art in heaven…""

I guessed we've all prayed emergency prayers in our lives, when things have gone wrong or when we need something really badly. Someone once said, that people often treat God like a celestial Jimmy Savile, for when we need things or are in trouble! Prayer, however, shouldn't be like that. It is simply communication with God. You get to know someone by spending time with them, and it's the same with prayer; you get to know God by spending time with him.

You'll probably remember from school assemblies reciting, almost parrot fashion, the Lord's Prayer. Why not spend a couple of minutes right now, writing it down and looking at it, because in actual fact it's a pretty good model of how we should pray. It's not surprising, really, as it's the way Jesus said we should pray. It starts with remembering how wonderful God is, it then talks about his provision and how we need him to help us. We then think of our sin and how God can help us with temptation. It really is quite a powerful prayer!

Telling Others

When something wonderful happens to you, you just can't help telling others. Good news is so infectious. When my children were born I was telephoning family and friends with the news, even though it was near midnight and I got into trouble from the nurses for using my mobile phone on the ward!

The story of Jesus is known as the 'gospel,' which means 'good news.' That's what evangelism (a technical word that simply means 'telling others') is all about, a very natural process of telling people the good news of what has happened in your life. Don't worry if you're not good at talking or don't understand everything the Bible says; God wants to use you anyway.

A number of years ago in America, an evangelist

called Billy Sunday was holding some special evangelistic meetings, and each night a young mentally handicapped boy turned up to sing with the rest of the choir. "Joey wasn't very bright," remembered the choir leader, "but he never missed any of the meetings and wouldn't leave until he had shaken my hand."

Near the end of the series of meetings a man came to the choir leader and said: "Thank you for being so kind to my son Joey. He's not right mentally, but he's never enjoyed anything so much as singing in the choir. Because of his nagging, my wife and five other children came to the meetings and have all become Christians. Last night his 75-year-old grandfather, who has been an atheist all his life, was converted, and tonight his grandmother also became a Christian. Now our entire family is converted!"

Don't panic or feel out of your depth if you don't know everything about Jesus, God and the Bible. You also don't have to get a sensible suit, a serious hair cut, a big black Bible to bash your friends over the head with or grow a beard! Just tell them of the wonderful change in your life, and tell it as it really is.

THIRTY-SIX

Is that the end?

WELL, YES THIS IS THE END OF THE BOOK, but I hope for many readers that this is the beginning too of an exciting new life through knowing Jesus. I hope you've enjoyed it, but much more than that, I hope it's made you think about God, Jesus, the universe and your part in it.

As I've already said, we can never scientifically prove that God and Jesus ever lived or that Christianity is true, though we can prove quite conclusively the facts of history, which we've already looked at in this book. Perhaps one of the greatest proofs for the existence of God, that I haven't really mentioned yet, is the change that Jesus has made and continues to make in people's lives all across the world.

For example, there are more Christians alive today than ever before in human history added together. Every single day 100,000 people world-wide become Christians, and 2,000 new churches are started each week. In the wonderful continent of Africa, 20,000 people become Christians every day.

In South Korea, home of the largest Church in the world, there are now 18,000,000 Christians out of a total population of 44,000,000—that's nearly a staggering 41% of the entire country. In China, 28,000 people become Christians every day, and it is estimated that in the last seventeen years, an incredible 80,000,000 have turned to Jesus. Things are happening at such a pace there are now more Christians in China than there are members of the Communist Party. Indeed some of China's most fervent evangelists are only aged 14 and 15. Exciting things are most definitely happening all across our earth. Lives are being changed for good! You can be part of it too.

Some years ago, in the hit movie, 'The Dead Poet's Society,' Robin Williams played the role of a teacher in an exclusive American prep school. On the first day of school, he takes his class of boys out into the hallway to look at the pictures of past, now dead, graduates of the school. He motivates them to learn and excel in life with the following words:

"We are not food for worm's lads! Believe it or not, each and every one of us in this room one day will stop breathing, turn cold and die. Step forward and see these faces from the past. They were just like you are now. They believe they're destined for great things. Their eyes are full of hope. But you see, gentlemen, these boys are now fertilising daffodils. If you listen close, you will hear them whisper their legacy to you. Lean in. What do you hear?" Then Williams says in a spooky, grave-like voice: "Carpe Diem! (Latin for 'Seize the Day') Seize the day boys! Make your lives extraordinary."

I personally found that movie really inspirational and I believe God would say to many of you reading right now: "Seize the day! Make your life extraordinary." You see, Jesus didn't come to give us rules and regulations, or to restrict us and stop us having fun. He came to give us life, and to make our lives extraordinary.

Thank you for your interest in this book and reading it right to the end. Let me leave the last words with Jesus himself who said this: "The reason I have come is to give you life, and life in all its fullness." That really is a life full of purpose, forgiveness, acceptance, meaning and destiny, not boring religion or a wishy-washy system of beliefs, but the real thing. That's real life through a wonderful personal friendship with Jesus.

For Further Study

Anderson, Sir N.	Evidence for the Resurrection (IVP)
Anderson, Sir N.	The World's Religions (IVP)
Andrews, E.H.	God, Science and Evolution (Evangelical Press)
Archer, G.	Encyclopaedia of Bible Difficulties (Zondervan)
Berry, R.J. (Ed.)	Real Science, Real Faith (Monarch)
Bruce, F.F.	The Books and the Parchments (Fleming H. Revell Co.)
Bruce, F.F.	The New Testament Documents: Are They Reliable? (Inter-Varsity Press)
Burrell, M.C. & Wright, J.S.	Some Modern Faiths (IVP)
Castle, F.	No Flowers...Just Lots of Joy (Kingsway)
Chapman, C.	The Case for Christianity (Lion)
Cotterell, P.	This is Christianity (IVP)
Field, D. & Toon, P.	Real Questions (Lion)
Gumbel, N.	Searching Issues (Kingsway)
Holder, R.D.	Nothing But Atoms and Molecules? (Monarch)
Legg, S.	Man, Myth or Maybe More? (Silver Fish)
Lewis, C.S.	Mere Christianity (Fontana)
Lewis, C.S.	Miracles (Fontana)
Lewis, C.S.	The Problem of Pain (Fontana)
Lucas, E.	Genesis Today (Christian Impact)
McDowell, J.	More than a Carpenter (Kingsway)

McDowell, J.	Evidence that Demands a Verdict (Campus Crusade)
McDowell, J.	More Evidence that Demands a Verdict (Campus Crusade)
McGrath, A.	Suffering (Hodder & Stoughton)
Morison, F.	Who Moved the Stone? (STL)
Polkinghorne, J.	Quarks, Chaos and Christianity (SPCK)
Poole, M.W.	God and the Big Bang (CPO, Worthing)
Poole, M.W.	Science & Belief (Lion)
Robinson, J.	Can we trust the New Testament? (Mowbrays)
Sayers, D.	Creed or Chaos (Harcourt Brace, New York)
Stott, J.R.W.	Basic Christianity (IVP)
Stott, J.R.W.	The Cross of Christ (IVP)
Watson, D.C.K.	In Search of God (Falcon)
Watson, D.C.K.	My God is Real (Falcon)
Wilkinson, D.A.	God, The Big Bang and Stephen Hawking (Monarch)
Wilson, R.D.	A Scientific Investigation of the Old Testament (Moody Press)
Young, J.	The Case Against Christ (Hodder & Stoughton)

www.reasons.org

Also by Steve Legg:

My Best Friend.
We all need friends. Whether we're boys or girls, or grown-ups. That's what this little booklet is all about—friends. In fact, one very special friend. The best friend anyone can ever have. Written by experienced schools worker, Steve Legg, for children aged 5 -10 years old, in full colour with fantastic illustrations from Jennifer Carter.

    CPO 3071—90p

Millennium Man.
Written by escapologist Steve Legg and illustrated throughout, Millennium Man takes a thoughtful look at the most extraordinary person in history—Jesus. In full colour and illustrated throughout, this 16 page booklet leads the reader to look beyond the traditional image of a white dress and sandals, to see ten aspects of Jesus' life that made him so unique. In Steve's laid-back but winning style, he explains who Jesus is and how to become a Christian in a way everyone can understand.
    CPO 373—75p

Making Friends
If you find evangelism and sharing your faith a daunting prospect, then Making Friends is the book for you. Writing in a straightforward, no-nonsense style, escapologist Steve Legg shows that the most effective way we can evangelise is simply by being a good friend to others and by being ourselves.

    Christianity magazine in its review of the book said it was 'written for the man in the pub.' It continued, 'no other book currently available hits the nail on the head like Steve's. With his conversational tone, wealth of human stories and airy delivery, he exudes a certain smileyness that reassures the reader that taking evangelism too seriously is a great crime, and that the only way it will work is if you 'be good news.'

Making Friends is an important and timely book. It takes us away from theories and seminars and back to basics—real evangelism, the Jesus way.

Silver Fish—£4.99

Man, Myth or Maybe More?
Humorous and easy to read, 'Man, Myth or Maybe More?' examines the person and life of Jesus, the most extraordinary man to have ever walked the face of the earth.

In full colour throughout, with contributions from William Hague, Mick Jagger, Gerald Coates, Cilla Black, Jonathan Edwards, Malcolm Muggeridge, Bobby Ball, Napoleon, Barry Norman, J. John and Billy Connolly to name just a few, it makes for a jolly good read!

"It's no exaggeration to say that my ambitions and goals, and the whole way I live my life, have their roots in Jesus' life and teaching. But whatever you make of him, there can be no doubt that he's influenced the course of human history more than any other person who has ever lived. To put it bluntly, Jesus is too important not to have a well informed opinion about. So read this book."
Steve Chalke—TV Vicar

Silver Fish—£5.99

Breakout!

The Breakout Trust is a registered charity, committed to communicating the relevance of the Christian faith. Its Director is Steve Legg—a Christian speaker, entertainer and writer.

Through humour and fun, Steve attempts to smash the misconceptions that many have about Christianity, and to show how faith in Jesus is not only reasonable, but very relevant and vitally important.

This he does in Britain and overseas in school, colleges, universities, prisons and out on the streets. Face to face, and through the medium of radio and television, he has reached millions across the world, and seen thousands come to know the reality of the Christian faith for themselves.

Steve can be contacted at:
The Breakout Trust,
PO Box 3070,
Littlehampton
BN17 5AW.
Tel: 01903 779 279
E-mail: steve@breakout.org.uk
or visit the web site: www.breakout.org.uk

"I thank God for your liberating message."
**Rt. Hon & Most Rev. George Carey,
Lord Archbishop of Canterbury.**

"He really is very clever indeed."
Mrs Legg, Steve's mum.

All available
from CPO!
Just Phone:
**01903
264556**
to order

111